Team-Building Activities for Every Group

By Alanna Jones

Rec Room Publishing

PO Box 404
Richland, WA 99352
(509)946-7315

Library of Congress Catalog Card Number 99-74244
ISBN 0-9662341-6-2

To my daughter Coral, who makes my team complete with her smile, laughter and beautiful eyes. I look forward to life as a part of her team in all the days ahead.

Acknowledgments

A special thanks to all my friends at Westside Church who played many of my new, crazy games and who make me feel like I'm a special part of their team.

A big thanks to Kim Cooper and Mark Inouye who invented wonderful, creative games that are worth sharing with the world. Thanks to Beth, Jeremy, Albert and all my other friends who gave me great game ideas to use in this book.

Contents

Disclaimer

The games in this book are designed to be fun and interactive. Common sense should be used when leading and/or participating in these games, and safety for all those involved should be considered. The author and publisher are not responsible for any actions taken by any person/s who leads and/or participates in any of the games or activities in this book.

So, have fun, be safe, know the limits of the members of your group, and always give people the choice of participation to insure a good time for all!

Introduction

Everyone is on a team! The people you work with, go to school with, live with, play with, pray with, and are born with are all your teammates in life. Some teams have a leader, coach, commander or boss who has been appointed to lead the group, while other teams are simply a group of people who must work things out on their own. In any case, most teams do things the same way over and over again and don't build more trust, confidence, or sense of purpose over the years. Instead, many teams start to fight, divide, and deteriorate until some outside source, event, or person puts them back on the right track and builds the team up to a higher level than where it was before.

The games in this book can be used to build any team into a stronger, more bonded group of people who are productive and confident with one another. Some games simply introduce new people to each other and create a fun and comfortable atmosphere for a group. Other games offer a challenge, build trust, and provide a chance for group members to communicate with one another. Whatever team you lead or are a part of can benefit from playing the team-building games in this book, and who knows — you may even have lots of fun in the process!

Building teams is a process just like building a house. When building a house, you must first build a strong foundation before putting the walls and roof up. Once the frame is standing, all the inside work like wiring and plumbing is done — work that nobody sees, but is necessary to make the house complete. Finally all the finishing touches go on and a complete, sturdy, beautiful house is ready to live in.

The foundation of a team is a strong bond, one in which every member feels like they belong, are important, and are valued by the other group members. When there are people in a group who feel like outsiders or like they don't belong, the foundation of the team is weak and it can crumble before people get the chance to build a stronger bond. A good way to start building this foundation is by playing games that include everyone, that get people talking with one another, and that mix people up so they are learning things about people they don't know as well as others.

The games in the "Mix It Up" chapter are designed to introduce new people to each other and to get people talking. The games also give people a chance to learn more about one another in a fun, non-threatening manner.

Once a group of people pass the stage of getting to know each other, they are ready to get crazy and comfortable with one another by playing games that make people laugh and have fun, and that include everybody. The crazier the game, the more the inhibitions of group members come down and the more people begin to feel like they belong. The games in the "Stir It Up" chapter can get any group laughing and feeling like everyone is just as crazy and fun as everyone else.

After playing the games in the first two chapters, the foundation of your group should be growing and becoming stronger. Your group is then ready to take on challenging team-building activities that build trust and confidence. Some groups may already have a strong foundation in which everyone feels accepted. A group like this is ready for the team-building games and doesn't need to "Mix It Up" or "Stir It Up". In any case, the games in these first two chapters are always fun for every team to play and can be used at anytime in your group's development as a way of loosening up a group of people and building stronger bonds.

Team-building games require a group of people to pull together their resources, strengths, and abilities in order to successfully meet the challenge presented. Communication is key and, for some of the more difficult activities, group trust is essential. If there was no trust before the activity, there will be afterwards — or there will be a great group discussion about why people don't trust others.

When leading team-building games, you may chose to either present the group with their task and then step back and allow them to work it out themselves, or you yourself may be involved in the activity. Some games require the leader to simply observe and to give as little assistance as possible, but some of the observations made by the leader can be great input into the discussion at the end of the game. When possible, it is a good idea for the leader to participate in the activity. This promotes an atmosphere in which everyone works towards the same goal and helps the leader to build relationships with group members.

All the games in the "Team Up" chapter have discussion prompts at the end. In many cases, the discussion after the game will be more beneficial than the activity itself. During the discussion, people will talk about how they felt when working closely with others, how they contributed to the group, how the game relates to their life outside the group, or how the game helped bring everyone closer together.

The type of group you are leading will determine what kind of discussion you hold after the activity. If you're trying to build a team out of a group of people who works together, plays sports together, etc., you will focus on the strengths of the group. Your discussion may focus on who leads, who follows and why, as well as how the group can apply what it has learned to the projects they have to tackle together on a daily basis. On the other hand, if you work with people who are trying to learn social skills or who are trying to bond so they can feel more comfortable sharing their feelings with each other (therapy, church, troubled youth, etc.), you will probably want to focus the discussion more on trust, communication, relationships, and how to apply what's been learned to life outside of the group.

A good discussion after a game can change how people remember the activity and how they react to others in the group. It also changes the game from a fun activity to a memorable learning experience. Getting everyone involved in the game is important, but getting everyone to participate in the discussion can be just as important. A good leader will gather the group together after the activity, sit them down in a circle or in a group, and ask leading questions. If there is a long pause of silence a good leader will allow time for group members to answer the questions and avoid talking too much. For some groups, the discussion can be very short and to the point. For instance, little kids may just need to understand what they just did and that they did a good job sharing or taking turns. Other groups may talk about one activity for an hour, and the activity will be simply a catalyst for a discussion of deeper issues. Whatever the case for your group, don't underestimate the power of a group discussion.

The discussion prompts at the end of each game are there to provide a guide for the leader. However, other issues may arise during the game that can be used to start a group discussion. You may simply ask the group what they learned, what they observed, or what happened during the game, and let the discussion go from there.

Most of the time, the discussion will occur after the game, but on occasion you may want to stop a game to hold a discussion about an issue that has come up or to help a team regroup when people have become frustrated or when they are having difficulty working together. Sometimes these middle-of-the-game discussions can address issues better than any other discussion the group will ever have, because if you talk about things while they are happening, people are able to gain more insight into what is going on. When talking about something after it happens, people aren't as connected to their feelings and thoughts as they were when it was happening.

Once a group has built trust and confidence by participating in team-building games, they are ready to "Open Up" and get into deeper discussions, to share revelations, and to affirm one another in a non-threatening way. Games are a great way to lead people to share more than they would if just sitting around in a group talking.

The activities in the "Open Up" chapter focus on talking and shar-ing. For some groups, the goal may be to get the group members to share feelings about the group itself, the workings, dynamics, and relationships of the people. For other groups, the topic of discussion may focus more on sharing feelings about what they have learned about themselves by being involved in team-building activities.

The games in the "Open Up" section come with discussion ques-tions as well, unless the activity itself gives the group the opportunity to share thoughts and feelings. Activities that give group members the opportunity to affirm one another and to focus on positive things are a great way to put closure on a group's time together and to leave the group members feeling bonded with one another.

Team-building games can be fun and beneficial for whatever team you are a part of or for whatever group you lead. Start simply by making everyone feel accepted and build a strong foundation. Build strong group support by challenging the group to work together and support each other with any task you give them. Finally, bring your group to a higher level with activities that promote discussion and offer affirmations and compliments. The games in this book will help you do all of this in a fun, interactive way for every group!

Mix It Up

Human Scavenger Hunt

Objective
To search for commonalities among group members and to get to know more about each other.

Group Size
12 or more (more is better!)

Materials
‐ A copy of the list that follows this game description

Description
Break the large group into smaller groups of about six to twelve people each. Have each group stand or sit together in a place that is separate from the other groups but of equal distance from you — the leader who stands in the middle of the room.

Read one item from the list at a time. The team who sends up a person or group of people to you first that fits the description you have just given earns a point. For example, you might say "two people who have the same middle name" and within each group the members must talk, find out if any two have the same middle name, and then quickly send those people up to you. The first group of people with the same middle name to reach you earns a point for their team. You may give a bonus point for different items if it applies — for instance, if a group has three people with the same middle name they may earn a point for this round even if they were not the first group to get to you. The group with the most points at the end of the game wins.

Team-Building Activities

Human Scavenger Hunt List

1. Two people who have the same first and last initial
2. The person in your group who was born the farthest away from here
3. Two people with the same middle name
4. A group of people whose ages add up to 100
5. Two people with the same birthday (or birthday month)
6. A group of people whose shoe sizes add up to 40
7. The person in your group who lives the closest to here
8. A group of people who have attended school for a total of 38 years
9. A group of people who can spell a word by putting together the first letters of their first names
10. A group of three people who all have different colored eyes

Variations

Ask for items such as "a 1982 coin" or "an expired drivers license" or any other items that group members may be able to find in their pockets, purses, wallets, or on themselves.

Add a stunt to each item on the list — for example, "Two people who have the same first and last initial must leap frog up to me"

Mingle

Objective

To mix up the people in the group, to have fun, and to create an atmosphere that is comfortable for everyone.

Group Size

20 or more

Materials

➲ A loud voice or amplifier

Description

Designate an area for this game to take place in and ask everyone to stand within this area. When you (or a selected person) says "go", everyone must walk around in the area (in no particular direction) saying "mingle, mingle, mingle . . ." until the leader yells a number. When a number is given, everyone must quickly try to get into a group of people that matches the given number.

For instance, the number five is called out then everyone tries to get into a group, cluster, or clump of five people (no more and no less). After a few seconds anyone not in a group is "out". Any group having more or less than the given number is also "out". Those who are "out" should stand outside the play area so they can still watch and enjoy the rest of this game. Keep playing until there are only two people left.

After playing one round by the above rules, play another round with added characteristics that people must group up by. A list of ideas follows.

MINGLE IDEA LIST

(Add a number to the beginning of each statement)

People of the same age

People who live in the same city

People with the same shoe size

People with the same eye color

People with a single letter that is the same in their first names

People who love to eat the same food

People who root for the same sports team

People who have the same favorite restaurant

People who have vacationed in the same place

People who have been in the same foreign country

Name Tag Grab

Objective
To get to know each other's names while trying to find your own name tag.

Group Size
8 or more

Materials
- Sticky-back name tags
- Marking pens

Description
Gather the group into a circle and hand out name tags. Pass the marking pens around and ask each person to write his/her name on one tag (don't take the back off yet). The leader then collects all of the name tags, mixes them up, and redistributes them so each person in the group has someone else's name tag (you can't have your name tag or the name tag of the person standing to your right). Ask the group members to not reveal to anyone whose name tag they are holding.

At this point, ask the group to place the name tag that they are holding on the back of the person to their right. On the "go" signal, everyone must move among the group members and try to locate their own name while at the same time trying to avoid having someone find his/her own name on their back. Once a person finds their own name tag they grab it off the back of the person who had it and place it on their own chest for all to see. Each person stays in the game until they find their own name and the person whose name was on their back finds his/her own name.

Since nobody knows whose name is on their own back, everyone should try to avoid having people look at their backs. The person who keeps the name on his/her back the longest is the winner.

Variation

The leader can collect all of the name tags and then redistribute them randomly on the backs of the group members.

Hello My Name is:

Eric

Sing a Song

Objective

To get people talking with one another in a group and to make group members feel more comfortable with each other.

Group Size

4 or more (more is better)

Materials

➲ A list of words

Description

Break the group into teams of two or more. (At least four teams with four or more members is best, but you can play this game with a small group as well.) Each team should be in a group and the leader stands in the middle of the room. The leader calls out a word (a list of suggestions follows) and then points to a group. That group has until the count of 10 to come up with a song that has the stated word in it and must sing that part of the song. At least two people in the group must know the song, and everyone who knows it must sing. Then the leader points to the next group, who has to the count of 10 to think of a song with the same word in it. If a group fails to sing a song before the time is up, they are eliminated. Continue around the room until there is one group remaining. You may want to count to five instead of ten to speed it up at the end. After the first round, select another word with every team back in the game at the beginning of each new round.

Word Suggestions

Walk	Love	Child	Up	Dance
Girl	Hot	In	Go	Sun	Blue

What Can You Do With This?

Objective

For people to begin to feel comfortable around one another and for everyone to give input when in a group discussion.

Group Size

4 or more

Materials

- ➲ Any odd objects you can find
- ➲ Paper
- ➲ Pens or pencils

Description

Select an odd object prior to the activity that can be used to do many different things — a stapler remover, a wire whisk, kitchen tongs, a strainer, or anything else. Place this object in a paper bag.

Divide the large group into teams and give each team a piece of paper and pen or pencil. Pull the object out of the bag and say, "Each group needs to make a list of all of the things that this object can be used for — and be creative!" Give a time limit. At the end of the time ask the groups to come back together and have one representative from each team share his/her team's list with the larger group. You may give points for each original item found on each list, for each item on a list, or no points at all and simply laugh at all the crazy ideas.

Personal Trivia

Objective
To learn interesting, little-known facts about each other so group members can become more comfortable around one another.

Group Size
4 to 20 (or a larger group can be broken into smaller groups for this activity)

Materials
- ➲ One 3x5 index card or small piece of paper per person
- ➲ Paper
- ➲ Pens or pencils

Description
   Pass out the index cards and pens or pencils to the group members. Each person must write down his/her name and five little-known facts about him/herself. Then collect all of the cards. Read aloud the facts found on a single card, but do not reveal whose card it is. At this point members try to guess whose card was just read. It is best to have each card numbered and ask group members to write down whose card they think was just read on a piece of paper next to the corresponding number. This way, when the last card is read, people cannot simply figure out who it belongs to through a process of elimination.

   After reading all the cards once through and allowing people time to write down their guesses, read them again and ask each person to acknowledge which card was their own and to give themselves a point for each correct guess.

Guess Who

Objective
To become more familiar with one another once everyone already knows each other's names.

Group Size
8 or more

Materials
- Sticky name tags or masking tape
- Pens

Description
Hand out the name tags and ask each person to write down his/her name on their own tag. Then collect all the tags, mix them up, and put one tag on each person's back without letting them know whose name you are placing on their back.

Each person must then mingle with the other group members and ask different people yes and no questions to try and find out whose name they have on their back. If you have a large group, only allow people to ask each person one question. Once a person correctly guesses the name that is on his/her back they may put it on the front of their shirt. If you need to get the group into a circle for the next activity, you may have them sit in a circle by sitting to the right of the person who is wearing their name.

Who Did That!?!

Objective
To learn more about each other and to generate interaction among group members.

Group Size
6 or more

Materials
➲ Paper
➲ Pens or pencils

Description
Select three people prior to the activity and ask them each to write down one of their most embarrassing moments. When the activity starts ask these three people to stand or sit in front of the group and then have someone else read one of the embarrassing moments. Ask the audience members to begin asking questions of the three people in order to guess whose paper was read. The person whose paper was read must answer questions about the incident truthfully, but the other two may lie in order to try to fool the group.

After many questions have been asked, ask the audience members to vote for the person that they thought the embarrassing moment happened to. After everyone votes, ask the person whom the story was about to reveal him/herself.

Several rounds of this game may be played with a different group of three people up front each time.

Name Game

Objective
For group members to learn each other's names.

Group Size
12 or more

Materials
- ➲ Paper
- ➲ Pens, pencils or colored markers

Description
Ask group members to break into small groups by finding people who have the same number of letters in their first name as they do. For small groups you may have to balance out the number of people in each group before the rest of the activity by moving people from a large group to a small group. For really large groups you may want to ask them to get into groups based on the number of letters in their full name.

Once small groups have been formed, instruct each group to first create a banner that contains all of their names. Each person must then find an object in the room that starts with the same letter as the first letter of his/her name. After finding the objects the group must work together to create a song, rhyme, rap, story, etc. that contains every person's name and each object that was found.

After all the groups have completed the task, allow time for each group to share their creations and present their story, song, rhyme, etc. with everyone else.

ABC Counts 1-2-3

Objective

To promote group interaction and work together as a group to complete a task.

Group Size

6 or more

Materials

➲ One bag for each team

Description

Divide the group into two or more teams and give each team a bag. Instruct the group to find twenty-six items, one item that starts with each letter of the alphabet, and put the items into the bag. The first group to gather all twenty-six items wins.

After this, ask each person to select one item from their own team's bag that they feel represents who they are as a person and to share this with their own small group. Each group may then select one item that they feel best represents their small group as a whole and share this with the larger group and explain why they chose that particular item.

One Common Goal

Objective
For group members to learn more about each other and find things they have in common.

Group Size
4 or more

Materials
➲ Paper
➲ Pens or pencils

Description
    Break the group into teams of two to six people each. Give each team a piece of paper and pen or pencil and ask them to make a list of all the things they can think of that are common traits among all the team members. Set a time limit for this activity. At the end of the time limit, ask each group to read their list to the rest of the group. For added fun and competition, see which group had the longest list and declare them the winning team.

SALTO

Objective

To interact, learn more about one another, and have fun.

Group Size

15 to 40 is ideal

Materials

- ➲ 25 chairs
- ➲ 5 sheets of paper with the letters S A L T O or B I N G O on them
- ➲ Sheets of paper numbered 1 through 25
- ➲ Tape
- ➲ Sticky labels
- ➲ Pens
- ➲ Chalk board or white board with writing instrument and eraser
- ➲ Small slips of paper
- ➲ 2 bags
- ➲ Paper

Description

This game takes some preparation but it is well worth the work in the end. It is a game much like BINGO (named SALTO after the youth group at my church). Prior to the activity make a list of at least twenty-five trivial facts about the members of the group and write them on individual slips of paper. Put these in a bag. On sticky labels, write the names of the people the facts are about. You will need one set of sticky labels with names per team. Each set of labels should be marked with a different color.

Set up the game by putting out five rows of five chairs, facing forward, spaced far enough apart for people to move between them. On the last chair of each row, place the large letters S A L T O or B I N G O. On the chairs in the S row, place a number 1 through 5. On the

A chairs, place numbers 6 through 10, and so on. Put the chalk board or white board up front with a large BINGO card on it that matches your chair set up. On small slips of paper, write the letters/numbers that correspond to the chairs: S-3, A-7, O-24, etc. Put these into a bag.

Break the group into three or four teams of five to ten people each. Give each team one set of sticky labels with names on them. These labels are "answers". The team members should divide the labels evenly among themselves and stick them on their shirts (each person should have more than one). Arrange the teams around the chairs.

To play the game call out a chair number (i.e., "S-5") then read a slip out loud (i.e., " whose birthday is on a holiday?") The group must work together to decide what the answer is, and the person wearing that person's name tries to sit in the correct chair before someone from another team does. Continue in this manner. You may want to write on the large bingo card which team occupies which space. Each team is trying to get five in a row. If someone is in a chair but they are wearing the answer to one of the other questions given, they may either try to move to the new chair or remain where they are in order to help their team get five in a row.

Four Corners

Objective
To increase group interaction, mix people up, and help people learn more about one another.

Group Size
8 or more

Materials
- 4 large sheets of paper
- Marker
- One die with the 6 and 5 covered up

Description
In a large room or gym, place one sheet of paper on each corner. Write a different number in each corner (1 through 4) so that everyone can see. To start the game, gather the group together in the middle of the room and point out the four corners. Read one of the sets of choices and ask people to go to the corner that best represents them (see list of suggestions). Example: "Would you most likely be found drinking: soda – corner 1, juice – corner 2, coffee – corner 3, or water – corner 4?" After the question has been read, everyone goes to the corner of their choice and once there they may talk about why they chose that corner with the rest of their group.

Once everyone is in a corner, roll the die (with the 5 and 6 covered) and whatever number it lands on is the "unlucky number". Everyone in that corner is eliminated and must move to the side. (You may also do a "lucky number" and that corner stays while everyone else leaves the floor.) Continue in this manner until a handful of people remain and declare them the winners.

Four Corners Choices

1. Would you most likely be found in a . . . sports car, luxury car, four wheel drive, or pick-up truck?
2. Are you most like . . . summer, winter, spring, or fall?
3. Would you most likely be found watching . . . the news, a game show, a soap opera, or a documentary?
4. Would you most likely be found drinking . . . soda, juice, coffee, or water?
5. Would you most likely be found in a . . . sailboat, canoe, yacht, or ski boat?
6. Are you more like a . . . potato, banana, bowl of spaghetti, or piece of bread?
7. Would you most likely be found in . . . sandals, bare feet, boots, or tennis shoes?
8. Where would you most like to go on vacation . . . tropical island, ski resort, amusement park, or campground?
9. Would you most likely be found watching on TV . . . golf, hockey, swimming or skiing?
10. Would you most likely listen to . . . country music, rock-'n'-roll, classical, or rap?

Group Favorites

Objective
To increase interaction among group members and to learn commonalities among group members.

Group Size
8 to 40 is ideal

Materials
- ➲ Question sheets (as follows)
- ➲ Pens or pencils
- ➲ Large chalkboard or white board with writing instrument and eraser

Description
Note: This game is played like the television game "Family Feud." Prior to the activity, pass out a survey (see suggestion) to the members of the group. (If you have a small group, you may want to survey people outside of the group as well). Collect the surveys and tally up the answers. Make a list of the top three to five answers for each question and rank them in order of popularity.

Break the group into an even number of teams with four to ten people on each team. Place chairs facing each other in two rows and ask two of the teams to sit in the chairs for the first round. The first person in the row of each team comes to the front. These two people face each other across a table that has a tennis ball or other small soft object on it. The chalkboard should be where everyone can see it, with the numbers one through three or six on it (this is the number of top answers you have on your list).

Now ask the first question (for example, "Name the top four favorite restaurants"). The first person to grab the ball gets a chance to answer the question. (If someone grabs the ball early, stop reading the question and make him/her give you an answer before reading any-more.) If the person with the ball gives an answer that is on your list, write it besides the corresponding number. If this person has not guessed the number-one answer, the other player gets a turn to guess. The person who guesses the highest answer on the list gets to choose whether his/her team will play or pass.

After this, each team gets three strikes (wrong answers). The team that is playing gets the chance to guess the remaining answers on the board. Give each person a turn. Once the playing team gets three strikes, the other team decides as a group what one answer they want to give to try to fill in one of the remaining blanks. If the first team fills in all the blanks they win the round, but if the opposing team guesses one of the remaining answers, they win the round.

Continue in this manner, playing many different rounds with differ-ent teams playing against each other.

Group Survey

1. Favorite restaurant
2. Favorite type of music
3. Favorite Christmas song
4. Favorite Shampoo
5. Favorite winter activity
6. Favorite celebrity
7. Type of car you ride in the most
8. Favorite place to shop (specific store name)
9. Job you most want to have:
10. Color of your toothbrush:

Name Balloon Pop

Objective
To become familiar with each other's names.

Group Size
12 or more

Materials
- ➲ Balloons (all the same color is best)
- ➲ Small slips of paper
- ➲ Pens or pencils

Description
Divide the group into two or more teams of six or more people each. Each team must select the person in the group who has the easiest name to remember. After this, each team sits in a circle and everyone (except for the person who was selected) is given a balloon, slip of paper and pen or pencil. Everyone now writes down his/her name on the paper, puts the slip of paper into his/her balloon, then blows it up and ties it. Each team piles all of their balloons in the middle of their circle and mixes them up.

The person on each team who had the easiest name to remember starts the game by selecting a balloon out of the pile. This game is a race. On the signal "go", the person holding the balloon must pop it anyway he or she can and then call out the name that is inside on the slip of paper. The person whose name was called then must grab a balloon and do the same. Continue in this manner until all the balloons have been popped. The first team to finish wins.

Candy Throw

Objective
To learn more about the interest and hobbies of group members and discover what group members have in common.

Group Size
8 to 20 is ideal

Materials
➲ 10 pieces of wrapped candy per person

Description
Have the group sit in a circle. Give each person ten pieces of wrapped candy. Tell the group that they may not eat any of the candy until the end of the game.

One person starts the game by telling the group something unique he or she has done, accomplished, or experienced in life. Anyone in the group who has <u>not</u> done the same thing must throw (or gently toss) a piece of candy at this person. Continue in this manner around the circle until everyone has had a turn. At the end of the game, players may eat the candy they collected.

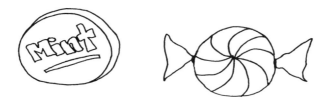

Stir It Up

Coop Ball

Objective
To help group members become more comfortable with one another by playing a crazy version of baseball.

Group Size
14 or more

Materials
- One six sided die
- Any variety of items that can be used to hit a ball (i.e. tennis racket, baseball bat, broom, etc.)
- A variety of balls or other items that cam be hit (i.e. tennis ball, baseball, rubber ball, teddy bear)
- Other items that you may need are a blindfold and/or helmet

Description
    This is a fun version of baseball that is called Coop Ball because it was invented by my creative and funny friend Kim Cooper.

    Prior to this activity gather up any balls, bats, blindfolds, etc. that you can find and create a list of six ways a ball can be hit, kicked, or knocked. Your list might look something like this.

1. Wear the blindfold and kick the purple ball (you may remove your blindfold before running the bases).
2. Hit the teddy bear with the tennis racket.
3. Hit the large rubber ball with the baseball bat.
4. Sing a song, then hit the tennis ball with the broom.
5. Put on the bicycle helmet, spin around ten times with the baseball bat touching the floor and your forehead at the same time, then kick the ball.
6. Hit the football with the bat.

Divide the group into two teams as you would for baseball and play this game on a baseball diamond or in a gym or field with marked bases. Play by baseball rules: three outs, if the ball is caught you are out, if you are tagged with the ball you are out, etc. When it is your turn to bat, you must roll the die. Depending on what number you roll you must follow the rules for that number. The person who is the pitcher must follow the directions and throw or roll the appropriate ball or object.

Variation

You may use a pair of dice and create a list of twelve ways to hit the ball instead of just six.

Marshmallow Soak' Em

Objective

To increase the comfort level in the group through fun interactive play.

Group Size

20 or more is ideal

Materials

- 2 bags of large marshmallows

Description

   Divide the group into two teams and give each team a bag of marshmallows. The play area should be a large open space with a line across the center to divide it into two areas. Each team is on a different side and cannot cross the line to the other side. On the signal "go" the members of each team try to eliminate the members of the opposite team by hitting them with marshmallows. If a marshmallow is thrown at you and you are hit, you must go to the sideline and get into line with your other teammates who have been hit. When a person on your own team catches a marshmallow that was thrown by someone on the other team, the first person in line may return to the game. The object is to eliminate the other team entirely!

Piggyback Tape Pull

Objective
To create an atmosphere among group members that is fun, wild, and interactive.

Group Size
8 or more

Materials
➲ 1 roll of masking tape

Description
Break the group into pairs and ask them to select one partner to ride piggyback on the other partner. Place a piece of masking tape on the back of each person who is riding piggyback. The tape should be about four inches long, and it works best to turn the end under so a tab is stinking out.

Designate a playing area that everyone must stay in for the game. On the "go" signal, each pair tries to grab the tape off of anyone they can while at the same time protecting their own tape anyway they can. Once your tape is pulled off, you and your partner must leave the play area and can watch the rest of the game from there. The game is over when one pair remains in the middle with tape on the back and with everyone else eliminated!

Bite the Bag

Objective

To increase group interaction and support of one another by playing this crazy challenge game.

Group Size

4 or more

Materials

- 1 large paper grocery sack for each team
- Scissors

Description

Divide the group into teams of at least two people each but no more than ten. Place one large paper grocery sack in front of each team, open and on the ground. Each person must take a turn trying to pick up the bag with his or her teeth. When trying to "bite the bag", you cannot use your hands, and the only part of your body that can touch the ground is your feet. If anyone falls over, can't bite the bag, or uses his or her hands, they are eliminated.

Once everyone on each team has attempted to bite the bag, cut two inches off the top of the bag. The remaining players now play a second round. Keep cutting the bag after each round and giving all remaining players a chance to try the shorter bag while their teammates cheer them on. The person who can bite the shortest bag wins the game for his or her team!

Newspaper Hockey

Objective

To mix up the group in a rowdy, fun, and interactive way.

Group Size

12 or more

Materials

- ➲ A large pile of old newspapers
- ➲ Masking tape
- ➲ Plastic baseballs

Description

Divide the group into two teams and give each team a pile of old newspaper and at least one roll of masking tape. Each person needs to take some newspaper, roll it up and tape it so it can be used as a hockey stick. Mark off a large area inside or outside that can be used to play hockey with two small goals.

The group is now ready to play newspaper hockey. You may play the game with one or more plastic baseballs. Each team is trying to hit the ball with their hockey sticks into the other goal.

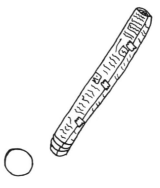

Water in the Face

Objective
To bring laughter to a group and for everyone to participate in a fun, interactive game.

Group Size
10 or more

Materials
- Paper cup
- Jug of water (or water source)
- Towels

Description
Gather the group into a circle where people can stand or sit. Ask for a volunteer to stand in the middle and give him or her a paper cup with a small amount of water in it. The person in the middle must select a category (i.e. type of car, color, kind of cereal, candy, etc.) and tell the group what the category is.

The person in the middle then secretly thinks of an item in that category (you may have this person whisper it into the ear of the leader so you know they won't lie). Each person in the circle takes a guess at what the person is thinking of in that category. Each person gets one guess and cannot say something that has already been said. As soon as someone correctly guesses what the person was thinking of, the person in the middle throws the water in his or her face!

The person who guessed correctly then gets to be the one in the middle with the water and may select a different category. Start with the person in the circle whose turn it was supposed to be next and move on around the circle until someone else gets water thrown into his or her face.

Pass the Present

Objective
To include everyone in a fun, entertaining game.

Group Size
6 or more

Materials
- A music source (radio, stereo, etc.)
- 1 or more wrapped gifts with many layers of tape and paper on each one

Description
Prior to the activity find a small gift. The gift can be anything from a candy bar to an old trinket you find in a drawer. Wrap the gift in many, many different layers of wrapping paper and make sure you use lots of tape!

Gather the group into a circle with everyone sitting down on the floor or in chairs. Start playing music and give the gift to one person, who must pass the gift to his or her right. The gift continues to be passed around until the music stops. Whoever has the gift when the music stops can start to unwrap it. Once the music starts again the gift must be passed around the circle until the music stops again. Keep going until someone gets to the gift.

The person who ultimately unwraps the present may keep it, or you may wish to use a box of candy or other item that can be shared with the entire group. For large groups you may want to have more than one present being passed around the circle at once.

Pull Up

Objective
To include everyone in a fun game that mixes people up while at the same time creating a friendly guy versus girl competition.

Group Size
30 or more (with a good mix of guys and girls)

Materials
- A music source (i.e. radio, stereo, etc.)

Description
The group must sit down on the ground in a large circle. Ask for three girl volunteers and three guy volunteers to stand in the middle of the circle. Inform the group that this is a competition between guys and girls and that the way you get a point for your team is to make sure that there are more people from the opposite sex standing in the middle of the circle when the music stops.

When the game starts, the music is playing and the guys and girls in the middle must each find someone of the opposite sex, grab his/her hand and pull him/her to a standing position, and then sit down in his/her place. This switching of places continues in a fast-paced manner and a person must stand when someone grabs his/her hand.

After a short time, stop the music and count the number of guys in the middle and the number of girls in the middle. The team that has the least number of people standing gets one point. Play several rounds of this game before declaring a winner. Start each new round with the people who are standing in the middle when the last round ended.

Pull Off

Objective
To help group members become more comfortable with one another in a fun and physical game.

Group Size
20 or more (with a good mix of guys and girls)

Materials
➲ None

Description
For this game, the guys must link themselves together in a tight group using their arms, legs, and hands. Once all the guys are in a clump the girls must try to pull them apart as quickly as they can (you may want to time this activity for added fun). Once a guy has been pulled off of the group, he cannot rejoin it or help his fellow man. Once all the guys have been separated from each other, the round in over.

Now the girls have a turn to bunch up, and the guys try to pull them apart in the least time possible.

Toilet Paper Wrap

Objective
To play a crazy game as a team that is fun and an easy way to start using teamwork.

Group Size
6 or more

Materials
➲ 1 roll of toilet paper per team

Description
    Divide the group into teams of three to eight members each and give each group one roll of toilet paper. Give the groups ten minutes to decorate one member of their group using the toilet paper. The person may be decorated as anything the group comes up with — nurse, sailor, statue of liberty, tree, etc. Encourage the groups to be creative and hold a fashion show at the end with each group explaining its creation.

Team Musical Chairs

Objective
To play a fun game in which everyone is included.

Group Size
8 or more is best

Materials
➲ A music source (radio, stereo, etc.)
➲ A stack of chairs (one less chair than the number of people in the group)

Description
Set this game up as you would for a regular game of musical chairs. Place all of the chairs in a circle facing outward with room for people to walk around the circle of chairs. There should be one less chair in the circle than there are people in the group.

Divide the group into two teams for this game. It is easiest to play guys versus girls because people need to easily identify who is on which team. Start each round with everyone standing in a circle around the chairs (spread team members out so they aren't all standing next to each other) and start the music. Everyone starts walking in the same direction around the chairs until the music stops. Once the music stops, everyone quickly tries to find a vacant chair to sit in. In this game of musical chairs no one ever gets out, but if you are left standing after the music stops the other team gets one point.

Continue playing many rounds of this game, giving a point to the appropriate team after each round.

Team Up

All Tied Up

Objective
To work as a team while your wrists are tied together.

Group Size
2 or more

Materials
- ➲ Bandanas or cloth strips
- ➲ Other items as needed

Description
   You may want to break a larger group into smaller groups for this activity. Ask group members to stand in a circle facing each other and to hold out their arms. Tie the group together so that each person is tied to both neighbor's wrists. Now that the group is "all tied up", give them a task to do together. Some ideas follow.

ALL TIED UP IDEAS
Make root beer floats for everyone
Wrap packages with gift wrap, bows, and a card
Eat lunch
Make a snack
Create an art project
Pour a cup of water for each person in the group
Complete an art project
Anything else that is fun and crazy

Discussion Prompts

1. Did everyone in the group help to get the task done?
2. What happened when someone didn't help?
3. Why were you successful (or unsuccessful) at completing the task?
4. Do you ever feel like you are "tied up" with someone else when you are working with them and trying to get a job done? If so, why, and how do you deal with this feeling?

Build It!

Objective
To build a structure as a group without touching anyone else's building materials.

Group Size
2 or more

Materials
➲ Building blocks (or other building materials)

Description
Prior to this activity, the leader builds a structure out of some blocks and makes a pile of the exact same blocks for the group to use. Show the group the pile and structure and then ask group members to each select one or more of the blocks for themselves until there are no remaining blocks.

Now the group must try to build the structure exactly like the original. Each person may only touch his/her own block/s and none of the other blocks. If at anytime someone touches a block that does not belong to him/her the group must start over.

Discussion Prompts
1. How did the group decide how to divide up the pile of blocks?
2. Was this an easy task for the group or difficult? Why?
3. What would have happened differently if everyone could have touched all of the blocks? Would this task been easier or harder?
4. Did you have to use patience during this activity? Was this hard or easy for you?
5. When in life do you need to use patience when working with a group of people? Why?

Reversal

Objective
For a group of people to work as a team when presented with a challenging task.

Group Size
4 to 16

Materials
➲ A large log or something similar to stand on

Description
For this activity you will need to find an object that is narrow but something the entire group can stand on. Some ideas are: log, bench, bleacher, parking lot curb, folded towels, a line of masking tape.

Ask the entire group to stand on this object and instruct them to completely switch the group around so that everyone is standing in the same order, only now on the other end. If at anytime during this challenge anyone falls off of the object or steps out of bounds, the entire group must start over.

Another way to play is to divide the group into two teams (boys and girls is easiest). The two teams must switch places on the log without anyone falling off.

Discussion Prompts
1. Did everyone in the group have to help out in order for the team to be successful at this task? What if someone chose not to help?
2. How did you feel about the close body contact that was needed for this activity? Did it make you more or less comfortable with this group and why?
3. Was trust involved in this activity? Why or why not?

Group Draw

Objective
To work together as a group to create an original drawing.

Group Size
4 or more

Materials
- Colored markers

Description
Give each person a different colored marker (or for added team-work allow the group to decide who gets what color). Give one person a piece of paper and ask him/her to make a squiggle or line on the paper and to then pass it to the person next to them. That person may turn the paper in any direction and add another line or squiggle. The lines must not intersect. The group should try to create a picture of something.

Once everyone has had a turn, ask the group to come up with a title for their picture. If you have a large group broken into smaller teams, hold an art exhibit at the end, allowing each team to share their picture with the rest of the group and to explain its title.

Discussion Prompts
1. How did you work together as a group to complete the picture?
2. Is everyone in the group happy with the picture that was created? Why or why not?
3. Was it harder to make the picture or to come up with a title? Why?
4. Is it easier to do things by yourself or with others?
5. Why is it important to be able to work with others?

Variation

Ask the group to work together to draw a picture, but instead of passing the paper around, they all work at the same time. All of the colors must be used, but each person may only use his/her color — no trading or sharing is allowed!

Pass the Clay!

Objective
To work as a team to build a clay sculpture.

Group Size
4 or more

Materials
- ➲ Clay, Playdough®, or other type of sculpting material
- ➲ Whistle or noise maker

Description
Break the group into teams of two to six members each and give each team a large lump of clay. Each team must sit in a circle so that they can easily pass the clay around. Start with one team member holding the clay.

The leader yells out an object, scene, or anything else that can be made out of clay (some ideas follow), and on the "go" signal the first person begins to build this as fast as they can. After a few seconds the leader blows the whistle and the clay must be passed to the next person, who picks up where the first person left off. Continue in this manner, with the leader frequently blowing the whistle at irregular intervals. On the "stop" signal, the person holding the clay must set it down. At the end of each round allow each group to show their creation to the rest of the group, with any description or story they want to make up about it. You may do several rounds of this fast-paced game with a different person starting with the clay each time.

.

SCULPTURE IDEAS

A bus stop
A popcorn stand
A clown
A barn with animals
A plate of spaghetti with meatballs

Discussion Prompts

1. Would this task have been easier or harder if you were by yourself?
2. Does being on a team make life easier or harder for you?
3. Did some of you get more time with the clay than others? How did this make you feel?
4. Do you ever feel like you put more effort or less effort into a project than other people do who are on your team? How does this make you feel?
5. What is the advantage of being a part of a team? Are there any disadvantages?

Variation

Give each person a different color of clay that they must add to the sculpture as they get it.

Have the first person start making something of his or her choice without talking. The next person has to continue the original sculpture when the whistle is blown. The group can't talk but tries to create something by the time everyone has had a turn with the clay.

Bid and Build

Objective
To work together as a team to build a bridge out of the objects your team obtains.

Group Size
4 to 20 participants is ideal

Materials
- ⊃ A large sheet of paper (or chalkboard, dry erase board, etc.)
- ⊃ A writing utensil for the paper, chalkboard, or dry erase board
- ⊃ Various items that can be used or not used to get a group from point A to point B (i.e. Frisbees®, sheets of paper, rope, hula hoops, pieces of wood or cardboard, an old garbage can, a tumbling mat, or anything else you can find)
- ⊃ Paper
- ⊃ Pens or pencils
- ⊃ Optional: Play money

Description
This activity is two teamwork activities in one! For the first part, list all the items that you have gathered on the large sheet of paper, display it for the group to see, and show them the items listed. Divide the group into at least two smaller teams of two or more and give each group a piece of paper and a pen or pencil. Explain to the groups that their task is to attempt to get their entire team from one side of an open area to the other side (at least ten yards apart) using any of the items listed and without anyone on their team touching the ground at any time.

First the teams must bid for the items listed. Each team gets 100 points (or $100 in play money) that they may spend however they wish on the items. They must divide up the points based on what they think will help them the most and write down their bids on the paper given to them. For example, one team may bid 75 points on the Frisbees, and 25 points on the rope. Another team may bid 50 points on the rope, 25 points on the Frisbees, 10 on the paper, and 15 on the cardboard.

After all the bids are completed, collect them and divide up the materials based upon the highest bid. In the example, the first team would end up with the Frisbees and nothing else, but the second team would get the rope, paper, and cardboard. If there is a tie for any item, you may have the teams bid again on certain items or divide the items up if possible.

Once the teams have their items, the second part of this teamwork activity occurs. They must now work together to get their entire team across the open area without any of the team members touching the ground in the process.

Discussion Prompts
1. Was it hard for your team to agree on what numbers to bid? Why or why not?
2. What did you do to come to an agreement?
3. When you disagree with others how do you handle it?
4. How do you feel about your ability to work with others after this activity?
5. What role do you usually take when in a group that is making decisions? Do you feel this is a good role for you? Why?

Variation
This activity may be done for an art project as well. Teams must bid on items that can be used to create a piece of art.

Blindfold Build

Objective
For group members to build trust in each other.

Group Size
2 or more

Materials
➲ Building blocks (or something similar)

Description
Blindfold half of the members of the group. Take out a pile of blocks and build a quick structure while the sighted people watch. Give the sighted group one minute to study the sculpture and memorize it. Disassemble the structure and place the pieces around the room.

The blindfolded group must now build the structure with help from the sighted group. However, the sighted group may not touch any of the pieces or any of the people when giving instructions. Once the sculpture is completed (or as much as possible), ask the blindfolded group to uncover their eyes and see what was made and inform them of how close they came to completing it, or let them know if they were able to successfully build the structure. Do another round of this game and have the two groups switch roles.

Discussion Prompts

1. Which role was harder for you? Why?
2. Did you ever feel frustrated during this activity? Why or why not?
3. Did you work as a team or as individuals? Why?
4. What solution did you find (if any) when attempting to complete this task?
5. What role do you usually take when in a group? What role did you take today?
6. How is this game like your life?

Circle Tag

Objective
For a group of people to learn to work together as a team.

Group Size
8 or more

Materials
➲ 1 blindfold

Description
Start the game by asking for a volunteer. Blindfold this person and ask the rest of the group members to hold hands in a circle surrounding him or her. The person in the middle tries to tag (or touch) those in the circle. The people in the circle must work together to avoid being touched by the person who is in the middle. If anyone in the group lets go at any time, the person in the middle wins that round.

Set a time limit (about twenty seconds) and challenge the group to go for this amount of time without being tagged. The group can try to get away from the person by getting the person in the middle to go under their arms and outside the circle without tagging them. After the twenty seconds, put another person in the middle and play again.

You may change the challenge by doing any of the following:
1. Blindfold two people who must hold hands and work together to try to tag the circle.
2. The person in the middle has no blindfold but has his/her shoelaces tied together.
3. Place a bell or other noisemaker on one person in the circle and challenge the person in the middle to tag this person while the rest of the group tries to keep him/her from being tagged. You may allow more time for this activity.

Discussion Prompts

1. What type of teamwork was needed for this activity (if any)?
2. Do you ever feel like a part of a team that is being pulled in many different directions? How do you deal with this type of situation?
3. What did each person need to do in this activity to make your team successful?
4. How did you feel when you were in the middle? Did anyone help you?
5. Do you ever feel like everyone else is on the same team and you are standing by yourself? How do you handle this situation?

Team Card Tower

Objective
To work together to accomplish a difficult task.

Group Size
2 or more

Materials
⮑ One deck of playing cards per team

Description
Divide the group into smaller groups of two to four people each, giving each group a deck of cards. Instruct the group that their task is to build the highest tower of cards they can.

When building the tower, each person may use only one hand and must place the other hand behind his/her back. The teams must start over each time the cards fall. It is a good idea to set a time limit for this activity and see who has the tallest tower once the time is up.

Discussion Prompts
1. What was needed from you and your team members to accomplish this task?
2. Was anyone frustrated at any time during the activity? If so, how was it handled?
3. How important would your teammate's help have been if you all could have used two hands?

Variations
Start with both hands, then halfway through switch to one hand and compare the difference.

Use your dominant hand part of the time and your other hand part of the time and compare the two.

Foothold

Objective
For the group to learn to work together as a team.

Group Size
4 or more

Materials
➲ None

Description
Break a large group into smaller teams of four to eight members. Each team must stand in a circle and select one person to be in the middle. The person in the middle can keep both feet on the ground, but everyone else may only keep one foot on the ground and the person in the middle must somehow hold or carry each group member's remaining foot (or leg). The challenge for the group is to move as a unit in one direction without the person in the middle dropping anyone's foot or leg in the process.

Discussion Prompts
1. Did one person have to work harder than the rest of your team for your group to be successful? Why?
2. How do you feel when you have to do more work than others who are on your team? Why?
3. How do you feel when others have to do more work when on your team in order to make up for you?
4. Is it OK for different people to work harder or less hard when on a team? Why or why not?
5. What are some teams that you can contribute more to than others in the same group?

Big Team Score Basketball

Objective
To include everyone in a team game in which players must work together.

Group Size
20 or more is ideal

Materials
- 2 basketballs
- Basketball court
- White stickers with the numbers 1, 2, 3, or 4 written on them

Description
This is a fun way for a large group to play basketball while using teamwork and making sure everyone is included.

Divide the group into four teams and give each team a batch of stickers with the numbers 1, 2, 3, or 4 on them. Each person puts a sticker on his/her shirt (team number one should all be wearing 1, team two should be wearing 2, etc.). Teams one and two will be shooting at one basket and teams three and four will be shooting at the other basket. Play with two basketballs and everyone plays at the same time. (It is best to play with no out-of-bounds if this is possible.) The object of the game is for everyone on your team to score a basket.

Play regular basketball rules, only everyone is playing at once and trying to help his/her own team members to score. Every time a basket is made, the person who made the basket takes off his/her sticker and places it on a score board that is on the wall (or have a person be the scorekeeper who wears all the stickers on his/her shirt). The stickers keep track of who has scored. Once a person scores one basket, he or she cannot make any more points for his or her team. The first team to successfully have everyone score a basket wins.

Discussion Prompts

1. How was this game different from a regular basketball game for you?
2. Did you get the ball more or less than usual and why?
3. Do you like to play team sports? Why or why not?
4. Is it always fun to play competitive team games? Why or why not?
5. What is the advantage to being on a team versus playing a game by yourself?
6. How can you be a better team member when on a team?

Variations

For a small group, play with only two teams and change the rules so each time everyone on a team scores a basket, the team gets one point.

Group Walk

Objective
For a group to build trust and cooperation.

Group Size
2 or more

Materials
➲ Bandanas, strips of cloth, masking tape, or an entire group who is wearing shoes with shoe laces

Description
Ask group members to stand side by side. Give the group bandanas, strips of cloth, or masking tape and ask them to tie (or tape) themselves together at the ankles (one person is tied at the ankle of his/her neighbor on the left and right, and so on down the line). If you don't have any ties to use people may tie their shoelaces together with both their neighbors.

Once the group is attached, ask them to work together to walk forward without anyone falling. If this is difficult for the group to do, break them into pairs and ask them to try walking with just one other person. Once successful with this, add another pair, so that there are four people in a group and try again until successful. Keep adding people until the group can all walk together without falling. If the group is very large, it is best to break them into smaller teams of no more than ten people each.

Discussion Prompts

1. How did you feel about your teammates during this activity?
2. Did you help each other or hinder each other during this activity?
3. What did everyone have to do during this activity to help the team be successful?
4. What happened (or what would have happened) if one person did not cooperate?
5. When in your life are you on a team that is dependent on you for its success?

Shoe Pile

Objective
For group members to build trust and communication skills.

Group Size
6 or more

Materials
➲ None

Description
Ask everyone in the group to take off his/her shoes and to put them into a big pile. Ask for a volunteer and blindfold that person. Mix up the shoes in the pile and ask the rest of the group members to verbally direct this person to his/her own shoes. The directions must be purely verbal without any touching, guiding or moving of the shoes. Once the person finds his/her own shoes he or she must put them on while still blindfolded.

For added fun divide the group into two teams and time each group as they guide their own team members through the shoes.

Discussion Prompts
1. How did you feel when you were blindfolded?
2. Could a person easily find his/her own shoes without any help from the group when blindfolded?
3. How was teamwork a factor in this activity?
4. How does this activity relate to your own life, if at all?

Back to Back

Objective
To learn to lean on one another for support.

Group Size
4 or more

Materials
➲ None

Description
Divide the group into smaller teams of two to three people each. Challenge each group to sit down on the floor with their backs to each other, link elbows, and then stand up without unlinking arms. Once a team successfully stands up, they need to find another team that was also successful and form a larger group together, sit back to back, and attempt to stand up all together. The smaller groups should continue joining together until the entire group is back to back and working together to stand up as one big team.

Discussion Prompts
1. Why do you think it is better to start this activity in small groups?
2. Was it easier at first or harder? Why?
3. Would you rather be on a small team or a large team? Why?
4. How are small and large teams different?
5. When are teams the most effective?

Team Four Square

Objective

To include everyone in a game and for people to work together as a team when playing.

Group Size

8 to 40

Materials

- ➲ Rubber four square ball
- ➲ Masking tape

Description

In a gymnasium or other large playing area mark off a giant four square game with the masking tape. Designate one square as the serving square (this is square number 1). The remaining squares are 2, 3 and 4.

Divide the group into four equal teams of at least two people each and have them pick a number between one and ten. The team that is closest to a predetermined (but secret) number starts in the serving square and the last team starts in square 4. Play a game of four square by the regular rules, only everyone is playing at once as a member of a team. Whenever the ball comes into a team's square it must bounce first before someone hits it, but anyone on the team can hit it. Once a person hits it, he or she cannot hit it the next time, but the time after that they can.

When a team is in the serving square everyone must take a turn serving before someone serves twice. When a team messes up (ball bounces twice, goes out of bounds, etc.) they must go to square 4 and all the other teams move up to the next vacant square. At the end of the game, there doesn't seem to be a winner unless you count the serving team, so it's all about teamwork and contributing to your own group effort.

Discussion Prompts

1. Was teamwork a factor in this game? Why or why not?
2. What things did you and your teammates have to do in order to be successful at this game?
3. Do you like playing games as a member of a team or as an individual better? Why?
4. What do you need to do if you want to be a good team member?

Line Up

Objective
To communicate with each other in a unique way.

Group Size
8 or more

Materials
➲ None

Description
Gather the group together and ask everyone to close his/her eyes (or use blindfolds). Instruct the group to arrange themselves into a line, using any of the following criteria. For an added challenge, give the group a time limit.

LINE UP IDEAS

Shortest to tallest
By birth dates
Number of letters in your full name (shortest name to longest name)
Number of people in your immediate family (smallest to biggest)
Where you were born (nearest to furthest)
Person who is newest to the group to person who has been in it for the longest
Anything else you can think of

Discussion Prompts

1. Did one person act more as a leader in this activity?
2. Is it sometimes necessary to have a leader?
3. What happens when everyone acts like a leader?
4. What happens when everyone waits for someone else to lead?
5. Are you more a leader or a follower? Do you like being in this role, or do you want to change? Why?

Teddy Bear Toss

Objective

For team members to work together instead of pulling against each other while playing a fun game.

Group Size

4 to 24 is ideal

Materials

- Blankets, sheets, or bath towels
- Teddy bear, or other soft object

Description

Divide the group into smaller groups of two to four members each. Give each group a blanket, sheet, or bath towel. Each person should hold onto a part of the blanket so they can toss and catch a teddy bear with it. At first the teams should stand close together and toss the bear back and forth. Gradually have the teams move further and further apart until the bear is dropped. If the bear hits the ground someone may pick it up, but otherwise there is no touching the bear.

Discussion Prompts

1. Was it harder the further away you got, or easier? Why?
2. What did each person on your team have to do in order for your team to be successful?
3. Was there any communication needed for this activity? Could you do this without communicating?
4. What happened if one person pulled the group the other way or let go of the blanket?
5. What teams are you a part of that require everyone to work equally? Do you do your part?

Variation

Play a game of volleyball by tossing a ball, water balloon, or other object back and forth over a net, using towels or blankets to toss and catch the item.

Piggyback Challenge

Objective
To build trust and communication skills.

Group Size
2 or more

Materials
➲ None

Description
Ask the group to get into pairs and for half the pairs to stand on one half of the room and for the rest to stand facing them on the other half. Each pair needs to select one person to ride piggyback on the back of his/her partner. The person who is carrying the other person closes his/her eyes. One the signal "go" the person on the back must verbally tell his/her partner how to safely get to the other side of the room without bumping into anyone who is coming in the other direction or who is on either side of them.

To make this activity more challenging you may place some other obstacles in the area that must be maneuvered around.

Discussion Prompts
1. If you were the one with your eyes closed, did you ever open them? Why or why not?
2. Did you trust your partner?
3. If you were the one being carried, did you trust your partner?
4. Why is trust important when working as a part of a team?
5. Are you trustworthy? Why or why not?

Lap Sit

Objective

For each person to do his/her part when working with a group to successfully accomplish a task.

Group Size

4 or more (more is better!)

Materials

➲ None

Description

This is one of the old favorites but it's still a good challenge for any size group! Start with everyone standing in a circle shoulder to shoulder. Now ask everyone to turn a quarter turn to the right so that each person is facing the back of the person to his/her right. If there is a lot of space between each person ask the group to take a small step towards the center of the circle while still facing right. Once you are in a tight circle you are ready for the lap sit. At the same time, everyone sits down on the lap of the person behind him/her. If successful everyone will be on his/her neighbor's lap and no one will be on the ground!

Discussion Prompts

1. Did everyone that was in the circle have to participate in this activity in order for it to work? Why or why not?
2. What happened if one person decided not to cooperate?
3. Are you ever in a group where one person doesn't participate and it affects the entire team? Are you ever that person?
4. How do you feel when you are part of a group that accomplishes a task that is difficult?

Can Walk

Objective
To work as a team to accomplish a goal.

Group Size
3 or more

Materials
- ➲ Large coffee cans
- ➲ Rope

Description
Gather together large coffee-type cans and punch two holes in the side-walls, opposite of each other near the closed end of the can. Place a thin rope through the holes and tie the rope in a loop that is long enough to hold onto when standing on the can. Make several of these for your group.

Divide the group into teams of two or three. Give each team one more coffee can than there are people. The teams stand on top of the coffee cans, holding onto the handles and walking. Each person shares the can with his/her neighbor so that they are walking together (with the exception of those who are on the outside edge — the outside foot is by itself on one can).

Once the group is successful at walking on the cans in teams of two or three, challenge them to walk in as big a group as possible.

Discussion Prompts
1. How did you feel when your group was walking together?
2. Was this easy or difficult for your group?
3. What would have made it easier?
4. What would have made it more difficult?
5. What made doing this activity as a team better than doing it by yourself?

Shake the Sheet

Objective
For a group of people to work together to accomplish a common goal, and to experience the limitations of working independently.

Group Size
4 to 16 is ideal

Materials
- Flat bed sheet, blanket, beach towel, etc.
- As many ping pong balls or other small objects as you can gather

Description
Spread out the sheet and have the group stand around it holding it as taunt as possible. Toss the ping pong balls onto the sheet and ask for a volunteer, who starts shaking the sheet while the rest of the group holds still and continues to hold the sheet. The goal is to get all of the balls bouncing. Add one person at a time to help shake the sheet and count how many of the balls are bouncing after each person is added, until all of the balls are bouncing and everyone is shaking the sheet.

Discussion Prompts
1. What happened when just one person was shaking the sheet?
2. How many people were needed to make all of the balls bounce?
3. Are you ever in a group where one person is trying to get things done and nobody else is helping? If so, what happens?
4. What is the benefit of having each and every person on a team help out?

Lighthouse

Objective
For each person to take on different roles in a single teamwork activity in order to support his/her team.

Group Size
4 or more

Materials
- ⊃ Various obstacles
- ⊃ Blindfolds
- ⊃ Pieces of wrapped candy

Description
Blindfold one person and put him/her at one end of a room or outdoor area that has various obstacles in it (i.e. rocks, cones, chairs, trees, etc.). Select at least three of the remaining group members to be "lighthouses" and ask them to stand in various places along the obstacle course.

Give the blindfolded person a handful of candy (one piece for each *lighthouse*). The job of the *lighthouse* is to guide the *cargo ship* (blindfolded person) through the rough waters (obstacle course) safely so that the *cargo* (candy) can be delivered to each *lighthouse.*

The first *lighthouse* must verbally guide the *cargo ship* through the obstacles and directly to the *lighthouse*, if this is done successfully the *ship* will deliver one piece of candy to that person.

The only *lighthouse* allowed to give directions at a given time is the one that the *ship* is headed for, but he or she may give support and encouragement after the person has gone past him/her. Any *lighthouse* whose area the *ship* has not come to yet must remain quiet until the *ship* reaches his/her area.

If the *ship* is put into danger by crashing into an obstacle the guiding *lighthouse* does not get any candy. Or, if the *lighthouse* is unable to guide the person successfully to him/her and the *ship* passes on by, then this person receives no candy and the next *lighthouse* takes over.

Allow the group members to take turns in the different positions. For large groups, you may have more than one obstacle course going at once.

Discussion Prompts

1. Did you feel safe when you were the "cargo ship"? Why or why not?
2. Do you think people in this group would have kept you as safe if candy weren't involved? Why?
3. Do you have people in your life whom you trust to guide you? Who and why?
4. Do you have people in your life who give you support when you need it? If so, who and what do they do? If not, why do you think this is and where can you go to find support when you need it?
5. How do you feel about the group as a result of this activity?

Variation

Put moving objects or people into the area the ship will be moving through to act as "floating logs". These objects or people should move through the area quietly while the lighthouses try to steer the ship around them.

Group Limbo

Objective
For team members to help one another when faced with a challenging task.

Group Size
4 to 12 is ideal

Materials
➲ Limbo stick or string and chairs

Description
Have two people hold the limbo stick two feet off the ground, or tie string between two chairs at this height. The challenge is for the entire group to move under the stick from one side to the other without anyone touching or bumping the stick. There are some rules that must be followed for this team-building activity.
1. The only part of your body that may touch the ground is your feet.
2. Once you move under the stick you may not return to the other side unless you successfully move back under the stick.
3. You don't have to go under the stick limbo-style, but you must never touch the stick.
4. If anyone touches the ground with any body part besides his/her feet the whole team must start over. (You may be flexible on this rule if you choose.)
5. You may help each other!

Once the team is successful at this height, challenge them to go lower!

Discussion Prompts

1. Could you have gone under the stick without help from your teammates?
2. How did you come up with a plan?
3. How did you feel if you needed more help than others getting under the stick?
4. Is it OK for some people on a team to do more work than others?
5. Are you usually needing more help than others on your team or are you helping others more?

Tall Tower

Objective

For everyone on a team to contribute to the completion of a challenging task.

Group Size

2 or more

Materials

➲ Varied (see idea list below)

Description

Prior to the activity, gather supplies together that can be used to make a tall tower but are not conventional things to build with. Some ideas are…

Paper (and nothing else)

Raw spaghetti and marshmallows

Gumdrops and toothpicks

Drinking straws and paper clips

Drinking straws and tape

Paper cups and a pack of chewing gum

String, paper cups, and drinking straws

Cookies

Break the group into teams of two to six members each. Give each group a pile of the supplies you have gathered and challenge them to build the tallest tower they can using only the supplies given to them. Give the group a time limit. At the end of the allotted time, ask the groups to show their creation to the rest of the group.

Discussion Prompts

1. How did you start this project?
2. Was getting started harder or easier than actually building the structure?
3. Did you have a plan or did everyone just start building? Was your group successful with the strategy that you chose?
4. Did anyone in your group emerge as a leader? If so, how did you feel about this? If not, do you wish someone had?
5. Could one person have done this project alone? What was the benefit of doing it as part of a team?

Variations

Everyone can only use one hand when building the structure.
Challenge the group to gather up anything they can find and to build a tall tower with these objects.

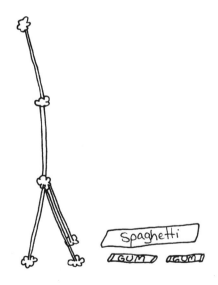

Three-Legged Sports

Objective
For people to work together and have fun doing so.

Group Size
8 or more

Materials
- ➲ Bandanas or cloth strips
- ➲ Various game supplies

Description
Ask the group members to divide up into pairs. Give each pair a bandana or cloth strip and instruct them to stand side by side and tie their inside legs together (three-legged race style). Once the group is divided into pairs, create two teams and challenge them to play one of the following games:

Kickball

Beach ball volleyball

Basketball

Soccer

Tag

Or anything else you can think of!

Discussion Prompts

1. Did you and your partner work against each other or work with each other? Why?
2. What did you have to do in order to play this game without falling down?
3. Was it harder to play this game with a partner?
4. Did you have fun playing with a partner or were you frustrated?
5. Are you dependent on anyone in your life for anything? Do you work with this person or against them?

Twenty-one

Objective
For team members to problem-solve and to communicate non-verbally with one another during an activity.

Group Size
6 to 27 is ideal

Materials
➲ None

Description
Divide the group into two or three teams of three to nine members each. Each team appoints a "counter" who will add up the number of fingers held up by the group.

Prior to giving the directions of the game, instruct the group that there is no talking allowed for the remainder of this activity, with the exception of counting by the team "counter." The "counter" may participate or watch.

Each team stands in a circle, facing each other, with their hands behind their backs. The leader counts "one, two, three" and on "three" each person holds out zero to ten fingers. The "counter" adds them up, and if all the fingers together equal exactly twenty-one the team has won the round. If no team reaches twenty-one, everyone immediately puts their hands back behind their backs and continues to play until one team comes up with twenty-one. Remember, no talking!

Discussion Prompts

1. Was it hard not to talk?
2. How did you communicate since you couldn't talk? Or did your team just hope to win through luck?
3. What happens when you are on a team and there is a lack of communication?
4. How do you deal with a group of people who have trouble communicating?

Cup Stack

Objective

For people to work together on a fun but frustrating and challenging task without giving up or cheating.

Group Size

6 or more (but you can do this with three people)

Materials

- Scissors

FOR EACH GROUP OF SIX:
- 10 paper cups of equal size
- One rubber band (must fit around a cup)
- 6 pieces of string

Description

Prior to the activity, cut string into two-foot to three-foot long pieces. Tie six pieces of string to a rubber band spacing them as evenly apart as possible. You will finish with a rubber band with six pieces of string attached to it (it should look like a sunshine with six sun rays going out in all directions). Make one of these for every six people.

Divide your group into smaller groups of six (or as close to this as possible). Give each group a stack of ten paper cups and one of the rubber band/string implements that you have prepared. Place the paper cups on the table, spread out and upside down.

Challenge the group to build a pyramid out of the paper cups (four on the bottom, three on the next row, then two, and finally one on the top). Group members may not touch the cups with their hands, or any other part of their bodies for that matter, even if a cup falls on the floor.

Each person should hold onto one of the strings that are attached to the rubber band and the group then uses this device to pick up the cups and place them on top of each other (by pulling the rubber band apart and then bringing it back together over the cups). If there are fewer than six people on any team, some team members may have to hold more than one string (but this does make it a bit easier).

Discussion Prompts
1. Was anyone frustrated at all during this activity? If so, how was it handled?
2. Why was teamwork so important for this activity?
3. Are you ever in a situation where you must use teamwork? Is this always easy for you? Why or why not?
4. What are some skills needed to be good at teamwork?
5. What is so hard about teamwork?
6. What did you do today to contribute to the teamwork on your team?

Take the Challenge!

Objective

For people to contribute their individual talents and skills to the group.

Group Size

10 or more (more is better!)

Materials

- ➲ Paper
- ➲ Pens or pencils

Description

Divide the group into teams of five to fifteen members each (the bigger the teams the better). Give each group paper and a pen or pencil and give them five minutes to come up with five challenges for the other groups to attempt to successfully accomplish. The group creating the challenge must be able to demonstrate that they can do it before another team is challenged. The challenges may be physical (build a pyramid, one person can carry five people, everyone stands on his/her head, etc.) Or the challenges may be anything else (our group has the most birthdays in one month, our group can sing any TV theme song you name, etc.). The challenge must not be obviously impossible for the other groups to accomplish (our group has the person with the longest hair).

Once the challenges are written down, each group gives out one challenge at a time and demonstrates it, then the other groups get a chance to try to accomplish this task in a given amount of time. You may give points to teams who can "take the challenge" successfully.

Discussion Prompts

1. Was it easy for your group to find things that everyone could successfully do? Why or why not?
2. Did you have to rely on the talents of the group members?
3. Did any team feel like it was hard to find talents within your group? If so, why?
4. How much do you rely on the talents of others or of yourself when you are in a group?
5. Do you always let your talents be known? Why or why not?

The Great Shoe Tie

Objective
For team members to help one another during a challenging task.

Group Size
6 or more

Materials
- ⮑ Masking tape
- ⮑ Optional: Rope or string

Description
Ask everyone to unfasten their own shoes. Instruct the group to stand in a clump as close together as possible (everyone's feet should be together and there should be no open space left on the ground at all).

The leader then takes the masking tape and makes a tight circle around the group on the floor, leaving no space for the group to move at all. Challenge the group to tie or buckle everyone's shoes without anyone falling out of the circle. (If anyone does fall out of the circle, the whole group must start over). If your group can do this easily, you may tie some rope around the group at waist level and give them the same challenge again!

Discussion Prompts
1. Did anyone feel uncomfortable with being this close to each other? Why or why not?
2. Did you need to help each other, or did everyone do his/her own thing?
3. Are you in any close groups that you have to work with? If so, how do you feel about this? If not, do you wish you were in more close groups?

Trust Tag

Objective
To build trust among group members.

Group Size
8 to 20 is ideal

Materials
➲ Blindfolds

Description
Divide the group into pairs and ask one person from each pair to be blindfolded. Designate a playing area that the group must stay in for the game and select one pair to be "it." Those who are blindfolded play a game of tag while their partners verbally guide them during the game. The sighted partners must keep their blindfolded partners safe and try to guide them away from the person who is "it." If your partner is "it," your job is to guide him/her towards the others.

Only verbal guidance may be given with no touching allowed (unless necessary for the safety of your partner or others). Everyone must stay in the designated playing area for the game. Halfway through the game, the blindfolded partners should become the guides and the guides become blindfolded.

Discussion Prompts
1. Did you trust your partner?
2. Was it harder to be the leader or the blindfolded person?
3. Do you have trouble trusting others or do you trust everyone?
4. Is trust important when you are working with others or in relationships with others? Why?

Swamp Crossing

Objective
To solve problems as a team.

Group Size
4 or more

Materials
- Pieces of cardboard about 1 foot by 1 foot (larger for adults and smaller for children)
- At least three 2-Liter plastic jugs filled with water with the lids on

Description
Break the group into teams of four to eight people each and tell them the following story: "Your group is stranded on an island and you need fresh water. The only water is in jugs on the other side of the salt-water, alligator-infested swamp. You must go and get it. You must do this as a group because the island gorillas are on the other side and are protective of their water but are afraid of a large group. You may use these special floating stepping stones (give them one or two fewer pieces of cardboard than there are people) that you can move across the water. The stones may be moved only by being picked up and set back down. You may not slide them because this will cause them to sink into the swamp."

Place the water jugs on the other side of the area and mark off a line that designates the beginning of the swamp and the end. Make the area large enough that the group may not simply make a bridge with the "stones" but must move the last one to the front in order to advance across the swamp. Remember, the group must bring the jugs of water back to the other side before the task is finished. For added fun you may put soda or other tasty drinks on the other side that the group can drink after bringing them back safely.

Discussion Prompts

1. Was this activity frustrating for anyone? Why or why not?
2. How did your group decide what to do next?
3. Was anyone more of a leader or did everyone give equal input?
4. What was the easiest part of this challenge? What was the hardest?
5. How did you feel when you had successfully completed the task?
6. Are you on any teams that have had to deal with difficult situations? How does this team handle it and how do you feel about that?

End Over End

Objective
To build trust between team members and to work together.

Group Size
10 or more

Materials
➲ Optional: a stiff plastic or metal chair

Description
Start by explaining the activity and then ask for a volunteer. The person who volunteers stands straight with their hands across their chest. The challenge for the rest of the group is to turn this person end over end and back to a standing position safely.

This may also be done while the person sits in a chair, only the person holds onto the seat of the chair while the group turns the person and the chair end over end.

Discussion Prompts
1. If you were the person who was turned end over end, how did you feel about this?
2. Did you trust your team members? Why or why not?
3. Did everyone in the group have to contribute? Why or why not?
4. Are you ever on a team where the safety of others is in your hands?
5. Are you trustworthy? Why or why not?
6. Why is trust important when you are a part of a team?

Knots

Objective
For a team to work together to solve a challenging puzzle.

Group Size
8 to 15 is ideal

Materials
➲ None

Description
    This is another old favorite that is easy to do anywhere, anytime. Gather the group into a circle. Each person holds out his/her hands into the center and grabs two other hands of other group members (but not two hands from the same person). Now that the group is in a large "knot," the challenge is to become untangled without anyone letting go of the hands that they are holding onto. The group should end up in a large circle, but on occasion it may work out that two circles form instead of just one because of the way people grabbed hands.

Discussion Prompts
1. How did you feel about the close proximity that you were in with the other group members?
2. Did anyone lead the group at any time or did everyone work on his/her own?
3. Do some groups work better when there is a leader?
4. Are you more likely to be a leader or a follower? Do you like this about yourself?

Footbridge

Objective

For two separate teams to figure out how to work together on the same project.

Group Size

4 or more

Materials

➲ 10 flat boards or pieces of cardboard (about 1' x 1' or a bit larger)

Description

Explain to the group that they will have to get their group from one end of the room to the other. The rules are that they can only use the boards given to them to cross the room. They may not touch the floor at anytime while trying to cross, but may step on the boards. Once a board has been placed on the ground it may not be moved (unless the group decides to start over and picks up all the boards). Also, once someone steps on a board, they may move forward but never backwards.

Divide the group in half and give each small group five boards (or enough boards to get half way across the room but no further when laying them down and stepping on them to create a "bridge"). Place the groups on the opposite sides of the room as far away from each other as possible. Ask them to devise a plan that will get their small group across the room while observing all the rules.

At this point, both groups will try to get across, which is very difficult because they don't have enough boards to make a bridge. Eventually they should figure out that the two opposite teams must meet in the middle and help each other to create one large bridge. Due to the fact that you cannot go backwards, there will be some teamwork needed to get around each other in the middle when teams are going in opposite directions.

This is a fun game. The less hints you give them, the better, and the further apart the teams are, the more effective the game!

Discussion Prompts

1. What was needed from both groups in order for this activity to be successful?
2. How did you feel when you had to cross paths with the other team in the middle of the bridge?
3. Are there ever times in your life when you must rely on others in order to be successful at something? When, and how do you handle it?
4. Is it ever hard for you to ask others for help? Why?
5. When should you ask others for help? Do you?

Group Skiing

Objective
For the group to solve a problem together.

Group Size
4 or more

Materials
- ➲ Different colored bandanas or cloth strips
- ➲ Old skis (without bindings) – can be found at yard sales and thrift stores or at least two wood boards (2"x 4"x8')

Description
Divide the group into teams of four to eight people each. Select a color for each team and give everyone on that team a bandana or cloth strip of that color. To make this challenge more effective, do other activities prior to this and tell the groups that the bandanas are to distinguish which team is which and to wear them for all the activities.

After playing other games, bring out some old skis without any bindings on them or some 2"x4"x8' boards and tell the group that they must use the skis to move their entire team across the "snow" (a distance of at least ten yards). The team may not touch the skis with their hands once they begin moving and the skis may not be slid across the ground; they have to be picked up and moved. Half of the group may go across at a time.

This task may sound difficult, but if group members use the bandanas to tie their feet to the skis it is possible to walk as a group in unison across the "snow"!

Discussion Prompts

1. How did your group devise a plan?
2. What part of this activity required the most teamwork and why?
3. Is planning something as a group harder than doing it alone or not? Why?
4. What is the best way for people to solve problems as a group?

Variations

Give the group a pile of stuff that is hard to use when following the above rules and crossing the "snow". Include the skis and bandanas in the pile and challenge the group to use anything they have been given to cross the snow.

Give the group rope pieces instead of bandanas.

Bowling Pin Touch

Objective

For team members to help one another work toward a common goal when another team is working against them.

Group Size

2 to 10 is ideal

Materials

- One bowling pin (or a plastic 2-liter jug with lid on filled one-third with water)
- As many different balls as you can gather (rubber balls, fuzzy soft balls, foam balls, or any kind will do)
- 4 orange cones or other markers

Description

Using the four cones or other markers, create an area that is at least forty feet by forty feet. Set the bowling pin in the center of the area.

Break the group into two to four teams and give each team the same number of balls. Challenge each team to touch the bowling pin with one of the balls without knocking it over. At no time may anyone go into the marked-off area! Each team tries to be the first to touch the pin with a ball and may try to keep the others from touching the pin with a ball by knocking any ball that has entered the area with another ball.

Before starting the game give the group the following rules: anyone can roll a ball at any time. The balls may be used to bump the other balls. Once a ball is in the area it may not be retrieved, but it may be bumped back out of the area to be used again. If the pin is knocked over, the whole group must start over with one less ball each.

The first team to touch the pin gets five points, and any team to touch the pin after that gets two points. Keep playing until all the balls are in the middle before starting another round.

Discussion Prompts

1. Did everyone take part in getting a ball to touch the pin?
2. How did it feel to have other teams working against you?
3. Did you want the other teams to fail? Why or why not?
4. Did you help the other teams? Did anyone from another team help you? Why or why not?
5. How can a group of people succeed while at the same time help others?

Water Transfer

Objective
To work as a team and use what you have been given when solving a problem.

Group Size
3 to 15 is ideal

Materials
- ⊃ 4 old bicycle tire inner tubes
- ⊃ 2 large coffee cans

Description
On a flat surface outdoors, draw a circle on the ground that is about fifteen feet in diameter. In the center of the circle place a can half filled with water. Give the group four old bicycle tire inner tubes and an empty can. Challenge the group to get the can of water out of the circle without spilling any of the water.

At no time may anyone cross into the circle with any part of his/her body. The extra can may be used for practice or for a bigger challenge — the group may try to retrieve the can of water and pour it into the empty can once it is outside of the circle. When pouring the water no touching of either can is allowed!

Discussion Prompts

1. How did your group come up with a plan of action?
2. Did the empty can help you?
3. What was the main thing your team did that made your group successful?
4. Are you ever on a team that must come up with a plan of action prior to starting a project? If so, why is the plan important? Does everyone contribute to the plan?
5. What was the communication process that took place during this activity?
6. How did you feel when your attempts failed? Succeeded?

Egg Construction

Objective
For team members to problem-solve when working together.

Group Size
8 or more

Materials
- ⊃ Raw eggs
- ⊃ As many different things as you can find that can be used to build an egg protection cover: drinking straws, tape, string, paper, card board tubes, Popsicle sticks, masking tape, glue, etc.

Description
Break the group into teams of four or more members each. Give each team a raw egg and tell them that they must not let their egg break, but they have to do one of the following with their egg (you choose):

Drop the egg from at least eight feet off the ground.

Drop the egg from eight feet up while your team lays on the ground below — with or without getting splattered on!

Make a pair of shoes out of six eggs (three per shoe) that everyone on your team can wear and walk around on.

Give the teams any of the materials you have gathered, or make a pile and allow them to select four items to use in the construction of their "egg protector." Once everyone has finished the project (or they run out of time), have the groups gather together and put their constructed egg protectors to the test!

Discussion Prompts
1. Was trust involved in this activity at all? Why or why not?
2. How did your group make decisions together?
3. How do you feel about your final product? Why?

Blind Square

Objective
To accomplish a challenging task using only verbal communication.

Group Size
4 to 20 is ideal

Materials
➲ A long piece of rope or string tied together at the ends to form a loop

Description
Blindfold everyone in the group and place the rope (with the ends tied together) at the feet of the group members. Challenge the group to form a square out of the rope. Once the group thinks it has created a square, allow everyone to take off their blindfolds and to look at what shape they actually created. You may do this with other shapes and letters too.

Discussion Prompts
1. How did you start this activity?
2. Did anyone emerge as a leader? If so, why — and why didn't others take the lead?
3. Do you tend to lead or follow when in a group? Why?

Variation
Videotape the group without them knowing it. Show the tape to the group after they are done and observe the different roles people took on during the activity.

Sneak a Peek

Objective
For each person to do his/her part when solving a problem as a group.

Group Size
4 or more

Materials
➲ Building blocks or something similar (i.e. Lego's®, Popsicle® sticks, etc.)

Description
Build a small sculpture or design with some of the building material and hide it from the group. Divide the group into small teams of two to eight members each. Give each team enough building material so that they could duplicate what you have already created.

Place the original sculpture in a place that is hidden but at an equal distance from all the groups. Ask one member from each team to come at the same time to look at the sculpture for five seconds in order to try to memorize it as much as possible before returning to his/her team.

After they run back to their teams, they have twenty-five seconds to instruct their teams how to build the structure so that it looks like the one that has been hidden. After the twenty-five seconds, ask each team to send up another member of their group who gets a chance to "sneak a peek" before returning to their team. Continue in this pattern until one of the teams successfully duplicates the original sculpture.

Build different sculptures for any additional rounds of this game.

Discussion Prompts
1. What part of this activity involved teamwork?
2. What did each person in your group do to help?
3. Why is teamwork important when working with a group?
4. What are some important elements of teamwork?
5. How can being good at teamwork help you in your daily life?

Variation
Give each team a pad of paper and a pen or pencil to take notes on for their five-second observation.

Have one person from each team look at the structure and then tell another team member what he or she saw. The second person may take notes and then go back to the team to relay what he or she was told. The person taking notes may return often for further instructions, but each person remains in the same role throughout the activity.

Push and Pull

Objective

For group members to figure out how to work together rather than work against each other.

Group Size

4 or more

Materials

➲ None

Description

Divide the group into pairs (the closer in physical strength people are to each other, the better) and ask each pair to face each other and to reach out their right hands. Each person grabs his/her partner's hand by making a C shape with their fingers and hooking hands with their thumbs loose.

The object of this activity is to demonstrate how people work against each other when they should be working together (but don't tell the group this). Once everyone is hooked up with his/her partner, tell them, "The object of the game is to touch your partner's right shoulder with your hands that are locked (no letting go)". Then say, "The way to win this game is to get the most touches, so make sure and count each time you touch your partner's shoulder". Most people will think that they are going against their own partners and will be pushing against each other, but really the team with the most total touches wins!

After one minute, ask each team how many touches they had total and declare the winning team the one with the most touches.

Discussion Prompts

1. Why were you working against each other during this activity?
2. Did any team work with each other to get as many points as possible? Why?
3. Do you usually work against people when you are on a team or with them?
4. What happens when people are working against each other but are on the same team?
5. What happens when people work with each other when they are on the same team?

The Really Big Puzzle

Objective
To use independent efforts when working toward a common goal.

Group Size
4 or more

Materials
- A large piece of tag board
- Scissors
- Colored markers

Description
Cut up a large piece of tag board into a puzzle with large pieces. (For a big group you may need to do more than one.) Give each person one or more of the puzzle pieces. Challenge the group to make the pieces into a puzzle with a picture on it. Each person draws a part of the puzzle on his/her own piece coinciding with what others are drawing on their puzzle pieces. You may or may not allow people to look at what others in the group are drawing. After everyone has finished put the puzzle back together and look at the picture that was created.

Discussion Prompts
1. Was communication important for this activity? Why or why not?
2. What did the group do when making decisions together? Was it an easy process or difficult?
3. What groups are you a part of in which members must communicate with each other?
4. Do you feel that you are good at communicating when in a group? Why or why not?
5. What does a person need to do in order to communicate well with others when in a group?

Group Jump Rope

Objective
For people of different skill levels to work toward a common goal.

Group Size
6 or more

Materials
➲ One very large rope (climbing ropes work great) or several jump ropes tied together

Description
Ask for two volunteers to turn the jump rope. Challenge the group to get as many people jumping at once as possible. The group may decide to have everyone jump in while the rope is turning. Or, everyone may start in the middle before the rope starts turning and it is turned for them to jump over. This is a problem-solving exercise.

Once everyone in the group has jumped once (if this occurs), challenge the group to jump as many consecutive times as possible as a group.

Discussion Prompts
1. If jumping rope is easy for you, did you get frustrated during this activity at all? Why or why not?
2. If jumping rope is difficult for you, how did you feel about this activity? Were others patient with you?
3. Is everyone who is on the same team always working at the same skill level?
4. What are the advantages and disadvantages of having people of different skill level on the same team?
5. How do you handle being on a team of people who have all different skill levels?

Our Hands Are Tied!

Objective
To help one another when presented with a challenging task.

Group Size
3 or more

Materials
- None

Description
Everyone takes off their shoes, places them in a big pile, and then stands in a circle around the shoes. Challenge the group to hold hands in a circle and for each person to retrieve his/her own shoes, put them on and tie or buckle them without anyone letting go of the hands they are holding onto!

You may do this in separate teams as a race for added fun and competition.

Discussion Prompts
1. Did your teammates work with each other or against each other? Why?
2. What was the hardest part of this activity?
3. How was communication a factor in this activity?
4. Why is communication important when working with others?
5. Do you feel that you communicate well with others? How does this affect your life?

Pile On

Objective
To build trust and team cohesion by asking everyone to work together on a challenging task.

Group Size
6 to 20 is ideal

Materials
➲ Any flat surface with edges that people can stand on (i.e. a large stump, desk, surfboard, piece of plywood, old shirt, bench, etc.) or a roll of masking tape

Description
Find a surface that is flat with edges that people can stand on, or make an area on the ground marked off with masking tape. The area should be big enough that everyone can fit in it but small enough that not everyone's feet can easily stand in the area. Challenge the group to fit everyone onto the area without anyone touching the outside area or falling off and to stay on for at least ten seconds.

Discussion Prompts
1. How did your group decide what needed to be done during this activity?
2. Did each person do his/her own thing, or was everyone working with one another? Why?
3. What happens on a team when everyone is doing his/her own thing?
4. What happens on a team when everyone is contributing to the problem solving process?
5. Are you on teams that work together or on teams where most people do their own thing? How do you feel about this?

Around the Corner

Objective

For two teams to work together without knowing what the other team is doing.

Group Size

8 to 20 is ideal

Materials

- ⊃ 2 buckets
- ⊃ Pieces of cardboard
- ⊃ 10 similar objects in two different colors (i.e., 5 red balls and 5 blue balls) that can fit into the buckets

Description

For this activity you need two adjoining areas — two rooms, a room and a hallway, etc. You should not be able to see from one area into the other.

To prepare for this game in one room, place one bucket with five balls (or other objects) that are all the same color. The bucket should be as far away from the door as possible. Now place "stepping stones" on the ground (pieces of cardboard). Place the cardboard pieces in a path from the door to the bucket spaced a couple feet apart. Set up the other room in the same manner.

Once the rooms are set up, divide the group into two teams and send one team to each room. The door between the rooms should be closed. Now, go into each room separately and tell each group that they must get rid of all of the balls in their own bucket and gather all the balls from the other room. The only way to travel to the door is to step on the stepping stones; no part of their body may touch the floor. No two balls may cross paths, and the only way for a ball to move is to be carried or passed between teammates from the team on the side it started on. Once a ball moves forward it may not move backwards. If any of the rules are broken everyone on both teams must start over.

The two teams must communicate with each other before starting if this activity is to work, but this they must figure out for themselves!

Discussion Prompts

1. Were you working against each other at first? Why or why not?
2. What did you need to do before you could start moving balls?
3. Do you ever start something without having a plan and wish you had thought things out first? If so, what happened?
4. Have you ever been on a team that had to work on a project with another team that was in a different place? How did you work together?
5. Why is communication so important when two teams must work together?

Survival Shopping

Objective
For a group of people to make group decisions together.

Group Size
2 or more

Materials
- At least one large store catalog or access to the Internet
- Paper
- Pens or pencils
- Optional: Play money

Description
If you have a large group, break it into small teams of two to six members each (or into as many teams as you have catalogs for). Provide each team with a large catalog from a store that sells a variety of items (such as Sears) or if you have access to the Internet, find a web site that sells a variety of items.

Give each team "money" to spend ($200 is a good amount). Tell the group the following story: "You and your teammates have been selected to spend one year in a space ship traveling to a distant planet and back. You will have one year's supply of food and water on your ship and you each will be issued two sets of clothing. Your team is allotted $200 to buy anything else you will need. You must agree on the items and cannot go over the allotted dollar amount."

Give each group some paper and a pen or pencil to make a list on. Set a time limit, and at the end of the time limit ask each group to report back with their list. Each group should explain why they chose what they did.

Discussion Prompts

1. Did everyone on your team agree on what to spend your money on?
2. If everyone didn't agree, how did you finally come to a decision?
3. Was it difficult to make decisions as a group?
4. What is the best way to make decisions when in a group? Is this easy or difficult for you?

Blind Creations

Objective
To build group communication and trust.

Group Size
2 or more

Materials
‣ Varies (paper and markers, blocks, Popsicle® sticks, Lego's®, etc.)

Description
There are several variations to this popular activity. One person creates a drawing, sculpture, design, etc. out of the materials given to him/her. The rest of the group is given a pile of the same materials and must work as a group to duplicate what the first person made by following his/her verbal directions. The person who made the drawing or object should not be able to see the group members and the group cannot see the direction-giver or the creation that he or she has created. You may allow the group members to ask questions or not. Once everyone thinks they have a copy of the original creation, allow both parties to view what the other has made.

Discussion Prompts
1. Was it easier to give or to receive directions? Why?
2. Would it have been easier or harder to do this activity individually, rather than with a group? Why?
3. How was communication used during this activity?
4. Why is communication so important when in a group?
5. Did everyone contribute to the project, or did a few people do most of the work? Why?
6. Are you ever in a group where a few people take over? How do you feel about this?
7. What can you do to help a group work together more effectively?

Points of Contact

Objective
For a group of people to communicate and problem solve when given a challenging task.

Group Size
6 to 20 is ideal

Materials
- None

Description
Mark off an area with two lines about ten yards apart. Challenge the group to get from one line to the other using limited "points of contact". A point of contact is any part of a person's body that is touching the ground (foot, hand, etc.). Allow the group a specific number of contact points (a good number is the amount of people in the group minus one to three depending on how hard you want to make the challenge). For instance a group of eight people might get five points of contact. The group must move as a unit, and once a foot or other body part touches the ground, that foot or body part can be used over and over again and it counts as only one point of contact.

Discussion Prompts
1. Did anyone want to give up at anytime during this activity? Why or why not?
2. Did you have to attempt this challenge more than once before you were successful?
3. What happens if you are on a team and you want to quit or give up?
4. Is the rest of the team affected by your actions when you are on a team?
5. How can you affect a team in a positive manner?

Puppet Show

Objective
For a group of people to pool their resources and to be creative when solving a problem.

Group Size
4 or more

Materials
- A table or large desk that you cannot see under (use a tablecloth or sheet if necessary)
- Paper
- Pens or pencils

Description
Divide the group into teams of two to eight people each and give each group paper and a pen or pencil. Each group needs to create a short puppet show to be performed for the rest of the group. Each person must participate in his/her own team's puppet show. The group must create the puppets out of whatever they can find (socks, hats, hands, etc.). You may or may not provide a pile of odds and ends for them to use. After a given amount of time use a desk or table for the stage and ask each team to present their unique puppet show.

For added team-building you may ask the group to create a puppet show about the group itself and to include any observations the team has about the group as a whole.

Discussion Prompts

1. Is it easy or difficult to be creative when with a group of people? Why?
2. What part of this activity did your group have the most trouble with? Why?
3. What part of this activity was easy and went smoothly? Why?
4. Was communication important for this activity?
5. How did your team communicate effectively with one another?
6. What is the most important element of communication when working with any team?

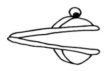

Flip

Objective
For everyone on a team to do his/her part when solving a problem.

Group Size
10 or more

Materials
➲ One or more large tarp, old sheet, or old blanket

Description
Find a tarp (or old sheet or blanket) that is large enough for the whole group to stand on while leaving about a quarter of it empty. (If the group is large, break it into smaller teams.) Once the group is standing on top of the tarp, challenge them to completely flip it over so that everyone is standing on the other side of the tarp. At no time may anyone get off of the tarp or touch the ground during this activity!

Discussion Prompts
1. Did anyone get in your way during this activity?
2. How did you come up with a plan with such a large group?
3. Did anyone emerge as a leader? Who and what did they do?
4. Do all problem solving activities need a leader? Why or why not?
5. Do you feel like more or less a part of the group after doing this activity? Why?

Big Shoes

Objective
For a group to build trust and cooperation.

Group Size
2 to 4 participants (or split a large group into small groups of 2 to 4 each)

Materials
- Two 2"x4"x6' boards for each team
- 2 to 4 pairs of large old shoes for each team

Description
Gather together two to four pairs of old shoes that are rather large in size. Firmly attach the soles of the shoes (with nails, screws, or strong glue) to the boards in such a manner that they all face the same way and one shoe from each pair is on each board across from its mate.

Place the "big shoes" at one end of a large area and ask the participants to put their feet in the shoes. Give the group the challenge of moving as a unit across the large area to reach the other end successfully.

Discussion Prompts
1. What did the group have to do during this activity in order to be successful?
2. What role did you take in this activity?
3. Are there ever times in your life when you must work together with others to accomplish a goal? If so, when, and what do you contribute?

Crazy Maze

Objective
To work as a team and to build communication and trust among group members.

Group Size
4 or more

Materials
⮞ Chairs
⮞ Yarn, string, or thin rope
⮞ Blindfolds

Description
Divide the group into two teams. Give each team a ball of yarn, string, or rope and a stack of chairs. Each team should be in a separate area or separate part of the room for this activity. Each group must work together to create a maze that can be walked through using the chairs, string, and anything else they can find to help them. The maze should have as many twist and turns as possible with some dead-ends along the way.

Once each group has created a maze, ask for a volunteer from each team who will be blindfolded, spun around a few times, and then given the chance to walk through the other team's maze. When walking through the maze the volunteer may get verbal help from his/her own teammates, but the team may not touch the person who is going through the maze. The other team may try to confuse the person with opposite directions at the same time.

You may try this with as many different people as possible, but the teams may need to change their mazes a bit between each person's turn to make it more challenging.

Discussion Prompts

1. Was it more difficult to go through the maze or to create one as a group? Why?
2. How did you feel when you were in the maze and getting many different directions at the same time?
3. Are you ever in a situation where people are all wanting you to do different things at the same time?
4. How do you handle this?

Ice Block Melt

Objective
To work together quickly and efficiently.

Group Size
6 or more

Materials
➲ One large ice block for every three to six people

Description
You will probably want to do this activity outside and in warm weather! Divide the group into teams of three to six members each and give each team a block of ice of equal size. Each team tries to melt their own block of ice as quickly as possible. The team that completely turns their block of ice into water first wins.

Discussion Prompts
1. How did you come up with a plan? Or did you?
2. Was it necessary for everyone in your group to help out? Why or why not?
3. What did you contribute to the completion of the ice melting?
4. Are there times when it is important for everyone in the group to contribute or the task will not be completed? If so, when?

Circle Walk

Objective
For a team of people to work together under challenging circumstances.

Group Size
6 or more

Materials
➲ None

Description
   Have the group stand in a circle shoulder to shoulder. Tell everyone to reach between their own legs, and join hands with their neighbors on both sides. The group will end up in a squatting position and connected in an awkward manner. Now, challenge the group to move in a circle to the right, completely around so that everyone ends up in the same spot that they started in — without anyone letting go or falling over!

Discussion Prompts
1.   Was this easy or difficult for you individually?
2.   Was this easy or difficult for the group as a whole? Why or why not?
3.   Do you ever feel like you affect what the rest of a group does?
4.   Is this a positive thing or a negative thing for you? Why?
5.   How do you use teamwork to overcome differences people have when working together?

Earthquake Escape

Objective
To build trust and to learn to work together in a situation in which people's abilities and needs are different.

Group Size
6 to 10 participants (or break large groups into small groups of 6 to 10 each)

Materials
- Cardboard
- Small flat wood pieces
- Cloth strips
- Cotton balls

Description
Explain to the group that there has just been a major earthquake and that many of the group members have sustained injuries. Select different group members to have different injuries and instruct them to act out these injuries during the course of the activity. One person may be deaf with cotton balls in his/her ears, another person is blind with a blindfold on. Someone may be unconscious and must lie on the ground. Others may have broken legs or arms with splints made out of cloth strips and cardboard or wood pieces, or you may tie someone's arms to his/her side. You may or may not appoint one or more people to have no injuries.

Once each person is set up with his/her injuries, tell the group you just got word that we are expecting aftershocks and they are in a dangerous area and must move to safety. Designate an area that has been declared safe at least twenty yards away. Prior to the activity, set up obstacles such as tables, overturned chairs, and other objects between the danger zone and the "safe area". The group must move everyone to the safety area without causing any further injury.

Team-Building Activities

Discussion Prompts

1. How did you feel when helping others get to safety?
2. How did you feel if others had to help you?
3. Do you have any disabilities that require you to accept help from others? If so, how do you deal with this?
4. How do you react to someone else who is working with you who has a disability that requires your help?

Balance Me

Objective
For team members to learn to give and accept support from one another.

Group Size
4 or more

Materials
⇒ None

Description
Divide the group in two. Both groups stands in a line, shoulder to shoulder The groups should be facing each other and about three feet apart. Challenge the groups to lean on each other and support each other's weight without anyone falling. Each person holds up his/her hands with palms facing the opposite team. Everyone must fall forward and lean on each other's hands for support. Each person's right hand should be on the right hand of the person across from them, and their left hand should be leaning on a different person's left hand. The people on the ends will have one free hand. All legs should be straight with no bent knees.

To make this more challenging, set marks of where they must stand. The group may practice in smaller groups and/or at a closer distance before attempting the challenge.

Discussion Prompts

1. Was this harder or easier than it seemed?
2. How was teamwork a factor in this activity?
3. How did the group go about successfully accomplishing this challenge?
4. What did you learn about each other as a result of this activity?

Motion Machine

Objective
To work together to solve a problem.

Group Size
4 or more

Materials
⊃   A variety of materials such as: paper towel tubes, toilet paper tubes, balls, string, tape, Popsicle sticks, plastic spoons, paper clips, pencils, fabric scraps, plastic wrap, sand, buckets, marbles, straws, cups, small toy cars, tin foil, etc.

Description
Divide the group into two or more teams of at least two people each. Provide the group with the pile of materials that you have gathered. Each group tries to make a "machine" that, once set into motion, will set other things into motion and so on down the line till the end. The challenge is to make the machine that stays in motion for the longest amount of time once it is started without any human intervention along the way. For example, a marble rolls and hits the spoon, which tips the cup, which dumps the sand, which moves the straw, etc.

You may divide the supplies up among groups yourself or you may allow the teams to take turns selecting items to use.

Discussion Prompts

1. Were you happy with what your group made? Why or why not?
2. Did everyone contribute to your team's project? How did you feel about this?
3. What was the process that your team went through when creating your machine?
4. What process do successful teams go through when working on building something together?

Water Carry

Objective

To problem-solve as a group and to deal with frustration if the task is not easily accomplished.

Group Size

4 to 12 participants (or break a larger group into small teams)

Materials

- 10 paper cups filled three-fourths full with water
- Cafeteria-type tray

Description

Prior to the activity, fill ten paper cups with water about three-fourths full and place five at one end of the room (or outside area) on the ground and five at the other end. The cups should be at least twenty feet apart from each other if possible.

Gather the group together in the middle of the room with a cafeteria-type tray placed on the ground and give them the following challenge. "You must retrieve all ten cups of water and place them onto the tray without spilling any of the water. You may only get one cup from one end of the room at a time. Before getting a second cup from that side of the room you must travel to the other side of the room with the tray and retrieve a cup from that side. When all ten cups of water are on the tray you must place it on the floor in the center of the room. By the way, each person can only use one foot and one hand for the entire duration of this activity and if any water spills the whole group must start over!"

Most groups will try to hop with the tray at first but this spills water. The best way to accomplish the task is to pass the tray down a line and for the person at the end to hop to the front of the line so that the chain can continue all the way to the end of the line.

Discussion Prompts

1. Did anyone get frustrated at any time during this activity? Why or why not?
2. Did you try different things before you came up with a solution?
3. Are you ever a part of a team and you just want to quit? When and why?
4. How do you feel when you are a part of a team and you work together to accomplish a difficult task?

Make a Meal

Objective

To problem-solve when in a group situation with everyone contributing to the project.

Group Size

2 or more

Materials

- ⊃ Access to a kitchen
- ⊃ A variety of food ingredients and food cooking supplies

Description

Supply the group with a variety of foods and ingredients that can be used to make a meal. Try to make the items random, but give them enough to work with. For example, you may give the group tomatoes, flour, salt, bacon, sugar, corn chips, pasta sauce, butter, lettuce, mushrooms, a can of soup, two eggs, and rice. You may specify that they have to use all of the ingredients, or you may let them use only the ones they want to use. Do not provide them with any recipe books and let them know what utensils, bowls, ovens, etc. they can use. Now let the group go to work to create a masterpiece out of the food they have been given. Of course everyone must try the food once it is created!

Discussion Prompts

1. How did your group get started?
2. Were there any disagreements along the way? Why or why not? If so, how were they handled?
3. How did you feel about the meal that was made?

Variation

Supply the group with specific ingredients for a meal or item such as cookies and allow them to work together in attempt to create the item they are told to make.

Sign Off

Objective
To work together efficiently to accomplish a variety of tasks.

Group Size
16 or more

Materials
- ➲ Paper
- ➲ Pens or pencils
- ➲ A variety of other items, depending on each challenge you choose

Description
Prior to the activity, create a list of challenges that can be accomplished by a group and assign point values to each challenge. You can use any of the team-building activities found in this book, such as Reversal, Circle Tag, Team Card Tower, Back to Back, Foothold, etc. Activities that can be done quickly with minimal set-up are best. Also have some other challenges on the list (your group must sing a commercial or TV theme song of your choice, everyone must whistle a song without messing up, find three objects with ten or more letters in its name, your team gets a point for each person who make a basket in a basketball hoop, etc.).

This activity works best if you have lots of leaders helping. Post the leaders around the play area and give each group of eight or more people a list and a pen or pencil. On the "go" signal each group tries to do as many of the challenges as possible. A leader must witness each challenge and sign it off once it's done. For activities that require props, you may designate a leader for that particular activity and give them the props needed.

Set a time limit, and at the end of the time each team must report in with their list. Tally up the points and declare a winner.

Discussion Prompts

1. Which challenge was the hardest for your group and why?
2. Which challenge was the easiest for your group and why?
3. How do you feel about how your team did?
4. Do you feel like everyone was trying his/her best at each challenge? How did this affect the team?
5. How do you feel after doing this exercise?

Variation

Set a time limit of five minutes or so for each activity and have the groups go from leader to leader, who will tell the group their next challenge. The groups change stations every time the whistle blows until all the teams have tried everything.

Lifeline

Objective

For a group of people to work together to problem-solve and to be resourceful when given a challenging task.

Group Size

5 or more

Materials

➲ None

Description

Create an area that is to be a "fast-moving river" by marking off an area on the ground at least twenty feet across (make it a bigger distance for larger groups). Ask for one or two volunteers from the group to go to the other side of the "river," Once the team members are across the river, tell the rest of the group that their friends have become stranded on the far side of the river after their boat tipped over, and the group must create a lifeline so that they can pull their comrades to safety.

The group must make a chain of items that are tied together out of anything they can find (clothes, shoelaces, tree branches, etc.). Once the group makes a chain, they must be able to hold onto one end and throw the other end to their stranded teammates. The lifeline must make it all the way to the other side when thrown. If it goes into the river it must be reeled in and thrown again.

Once the lifeline reaches the other side, the teammates may be pulled to safety one at a time.

Discussion Prompts

1. Did everyone contribute to the lifeline? Why or why not?
2. Could one person have made the lifeline? Why or why not?
3. Would you want to be across a real river and be depending on this group to throw you a lifeline? Why or why not?
4. If this was a real river, how would trust be a factor?

Totem Pole Tower

Objective

For each person to contribute his/her own unique qualities to a group project.

Group Size

5 or more

Materials

- ➲ One toilet paper tube per person
- ➲ Masking tape
- ➲ Colored markers
- ➲ Paper
- ➲ Pens or pencils
- ➲ Optional: colored paper, glue, pipe cleaners, yarn, straws, etc.

Description

Divide a large group into smaller teams of five to eight members each. Give each person one cardboard toilet paper tube and provide each team with colored markers, masking tape, paper, a pen or pencil, and anything else you have gathered.

Each person must create an animal on his/her own toilet paper roll. Each team must build a totem pole out of the animals made by its team members. Once the totem pole is made, the group must work together to create a story that is told about the animals on their pole.

Allow time at the end for each group to share their totem pole and to tell the story they have written.

Discussion Prompts

1. Do you like working by yourself and then adding your part to the group project, or do you prefer to work with others on a project? Why?
2. What was the most difficult part of this project? Why?
3. Do you compare your work to what others have made? Why or why not?
4. How do you feel about the end product?
5. How does your totem pole and story represent your group?

Variation

Ask each person to select an animal that best represents how they see themselves and to work together as a group to create a totem pole and write a story about these animals.

Sand Castles

Objective

For each person on a team to work hard to get a project completed before the time is up and then for the team to work together to protect the project.

Group Size

12 or more

Materials

- A sandy beach (or area)
- Water
- Buckets
- Shovels
- Water balloons
- Rubber surgical tubing
- Bandanas, pieces of cloth, funnels, or paint filters

Description

Find an area with a sandy beach where teams can spread out. Break groups into teams of six or more people each and give each team at least one bucket and one shovel. The teams should be spaced apart at equal distances. Give the group a certain amount of time to build their sand castles. Inform the teams that each castle may come under attack, so it must be built strong enough to withstand being bombarded by water balloons. In order to win the attack, it must be the largest castle left standing when the bombardment is over!

After the teams have built their sand castles, give each team as many water balloons as possible, some surgical tubing and a bandana, cloth strip, funnel, or paint filter. Tell them the attack will start in ten minutes, and each team must make a sling shot out of what you have given them. Once the time limit is up, the attack begins. Each team may use only their sling shot when trying to destroy the other castles, and they must stay behind their own castle when launching their water balloons. You may or may not allow people to block incoming water balloons. Once everyone is out of balloons, the attack is over. You may hold an inspection of the castles for fun.

Discussion Prompts

1. Did building the sand castle or the sling shot require more teamwork? Why?
2. How did you feel when your sand castle got hit by balloons?
3. How did your team use teamwork most effectively during this activity?

Shoe Tie You Bother Me

Objective
For people to help one another and to build communication and problem-solving skills among group members.

Group Size
8 or more

Materials
➲ None

Description
Divide the group into two or more teams with at least four people on each team. Everyone must lie on the floor as a group with legs in the air (no wearing skirts or dresses for this one!). On the "go" signal, each team tries to get all of the shoes on their team untied before one of the other teams does. No using hands during this activity, and your feet must stay off of the ground. (If anyone has a double knot in his/her shoe it may be untied before the game begins.)

Discussion Prompts
1. Was this activity frustrating for anyone? If so, how did your teammates help you?
2. Could you have done this challenge by yourself? Why or why not?
3. What did you do to help each other?
4. Are you on any teams in your life in which you rely on others for help and others rely on you? If so, does your team help each other or work against each other? If not, would you like to be on this kind of team?

Open Up

Who Are You at the Zoo?

Objective
To explore how people are feeling as individuals and as a part of a group.

Group Size
4 to 10 (or a larger group may be broken into smaller groups)

Materials
- 1 large sheet of white paper for each group
- Colored markers, crayons, or colored pencils
- Optional: colored paper, glue, yarn, glitter, ribbons, scissors, tape

Description
   Divide a large group into smaller groups of ten or less people each and give each group a large sheet of white paper, colored markers and/or anything else you have gathered together.

   Each group needs to work together to create a zoo on the large piece of paper using the materials they have been given. The zoo should be given a name that reflects the characteristics of the group. Each person needs to select an animal or person (zoo keeper, popcorn vendor, animal cage-cleaner, etc.) who is found at the zoo that represents how they see themselves.

   You may be very specific with your directions about what the animal or character represents based upon your group. For a church group you may select animals that represent your relationship with God; for a corporate group you may look for things that represent how you feel when at work; or for a therapy group you may pick animals that represent your emotional state or relationship with others. Each person should draw or place his/her own animal on the paper drawing of the zoo.

Ask each person to explain their choice of animal or person and to write this down or verbally share it with the rest of the group. If you have more than one small group, allow time for each group to share their creations with the rest of the group.

Discussion Prompts

1. What did you learn about yourself while doing this activity?
2. What did you learn about the group or about other members of the group today?
3. Is there a different animal or person that you would rather be? Why or why not?

Pile of Hats

Objective
For people to share how they feel and to recognize how they act or feel when around different groups of people.

Group Size
2 to 20

Materials
⊃   A large pile of hats of many different shapes and sizes

Description
Gather together as many different and unique kinds of hats as you can find and place them in the center of the room. Ask the group members to sit in a circle around the hats and select one member of the group to start. Ask this person to choose the one hat that they feel best represents how they are feeling right now. Allow everyone to take a turn selecting a hat and to explain why they chose the hat that they did. Each person should return his/her hat to the pile when their turn is done so others may select the same hat if they choose.

After everyone has chosen a hat, the group may do more rounds of this activity with different instructions. You may ask them to select a hat that represents how they feel when with this group, when with their family, when alone, when at school, when at work, etc. Compare the different "hats" people wear when with different groups.

Discussion Prompts
1.   Do you think it's good to wear different "hats" when in different situations, or do you wish you could always be the same?
2.   Do you wish any of the hats you chose today were different? Why?
3.   If you could only wear one hat all the time, which one would it be and why?

Group Symbols

Objective

For group members to talk about the strengths and weaknesses they possess and to recognize the strengths and weaknesses of the whole group.

Group Size

2 or more

Materials

➲ None

Description

Each person in the group must find something to symbolize how they see the group. They are to then find something else that represents their individual role in the group. The objects can be something that can be held in their hand, or they can be something nearby that can be pointed to (clouds, trees, lights, buildings, etc.). Allow enough time for everyone to find both symbols. A great way to do this is to go for a walk as a group.

Once everyone has collected two things, bring the group together and ask each person to share what they have collected with the group and to explain its meaning.

Discussion Prompts

Discuss each symbol after it has been shared by allowing people to ask questions about what each person shares.

Snowball Fight

Objective
For group members to share their thoughts and feelings with each other anonymously.

Group Size
8 or more is ideal

Materials
- Paper
- Pens or pencils

Description
Give everyone a piece of paper and a pen or pencil. Ask them to write down something specific on this piece of paper that you want them to share but that may be difficult to share, such as:

How you feel when with this group?
How are you feeling right now?
What do you do when you become really angry?
What makes you feel really sad?
What are the strengths and weaknesses of this group?

Make sure nobody puts his/her name on the papers because everything should be anonymous. Once everyone has finished writing, tell the group that they will be having a snowball fight and to crumple up their papers and, on the count of three, start throwing. After the snowball fight has gone on for a while, yell "stop," and ask each person to pick up one "snowball." Gather the group together and ask group members to take turns reading the paper that they ended up with to the group. You may discuss each response that is read or wait until all the papers have been read before having a discussion.

Discussion Prompts

1. What did you hear that surprised you?
2. How do you feel about what people shared today?
3. How did you feel about the way you shared your feelings?
4. Does anyone want to comment on or add to what was said?

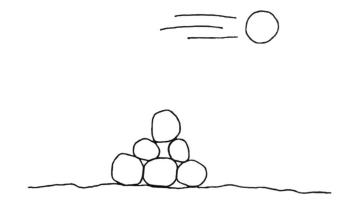

Shoes and Footprints

Objective
To talk about how group members (or the group as a whole) are doing currently, where they been and where they are going.

Group Size
1 or more

Materials
- A black-and-white drawing of a shoe
- A black-and-white drawing of a footprint
- Paper
- Pens or pencils

Description
Prior to the activity, find or make a simple black-and-white drawing of a shoe and make copies for everyone in the group. Also find a picture of a footprint and make copies of this for group members.

Give each person in the group a copy of the shoe picture and a pen or pencil. Ask group members to write on the sole of their shoe how their soul is really feeling right now. On the tongue they should write how they say they are feeling when they talk to others. On the back part they should write something that is giving them support and keeping them strong.

After everyone has completed their shoe picture, give each person a picture of a footprint and ask them to write down how they used to be and what kind of footprint they have left behind. Then give everyone a blank piece of paper and tell them, "This is a spot in the earth that will one day bear your footprint. What do you want your footprint to say about you?"

Allow time at the end for everyone to share as much of what they have written down as they feel comfortable sharing.

Discussion Prompts

1. What kind of journey is your life taking?
2. How do you feel about the "footprints" you are leaving behind?
3. What kind of "footprints" do you want to leave in the path ahead?

Variation

Instead of asking group members to answer the questions about themselves, have them answer the questions about the group as a whole.

Group Sculptures

Objective

To learn how different members of the group view the dynamics of the group.

Group Size

6 or more

Materials

- None

Description

Group members take turns "sculpting" the other group members into a life-size sculpture that represents how they see the group dynamics and personalities.

When it is your turn, you may position each person in a pose or place in relation to the others in the group. Once everyone is in place, the person who put them there explains why they see the group that way. For example someone might group three friends together and put others spread out across the room and explain that the three people are so close that others feel left out. The next person may see the group dynamics totally differently and have those three people mixed in with others in the group or spread apart.

For small groups give everyone a chance to make a sculpture, but for larger groups you may have a handful of people create sculptures and then ask for input after each one.

Discussion Prompts

1. Why do people see the group differently?
2. Do you feel this was a healthy activity for the group to do? Why or why not?
3. How do group dynamics affect a team?
4. What if everyone on the team was exactly the same?
5. What are the positive dynamics of this group?

Variation

The "sculpture" may be made out of items such as pieces of candy, stuffed animals, crayons, etc. People may choose particular items from the group of items that they feel represents each person and arrange them into a sculpture.

Bridge

Objective
For each person to contribute his/her strengths to the group.

Group Size
4 or more

Materials
- Paper plates
- Black markers

Description
Give the group a stack of paper plates and a few black markers. The group, should have enough paper plates to make a "stepping stone bridge" across the room or play area.

Don't tell the group that they will be making a bridge. Simply ask them to each take a paper plate and write down one of their own strengths, attributes, or talents on it. Tell them that they can do this on more than one plate if they feel they have more than one strength.

After the group members feel that they have written down as many strengths as they have, tell them they must use the paper plates to make a bridge across the room. When building the bridge and when crossing the room, the only plates that the group can use are ones with strengths written down on them. At no time may anyone's feet touch the floor. If the group needs to add more plates to the bridge, people must write down more strengths on more plates and add them to the bridge.

Discussion Prompts

1. Could one person build a bridge by themselves? Why or why not?
2. How is a group enhanced when there are many different people working on the same team?
3. What strengths did group members not write down that you felt they should have?
4. Each individual on the team has many strengths, as we can see. What strengths do you think this group has as a whole?

Leader

Listener

Strong

Organized

Humor

Creative

Award Ceremony

Objective
For group members to affirm one another.

Group Size
2 or more

Materials
- A large stack of old newspapers

Description
Put stacks of old newspapers in the middle of the floor and have group members sit in a circle around them. Tell the group that each person must create a trophy for the person on his/her right. The trophy should be made out of newspaper and reflect the positive qualities of the person it is for. People may fold, crumple, or tear the newspaper to create the trophy.

Once everyone has created a trophy for the person on his/her right, hold an award ceremony. One person at a time stands up and explains what the trophy is, who it is for, and why this person deserves this award.

Discussion Prompts
1. How does it feel to be recognized for the good things that you do?
2. How does it feel to give compliments to others? Why don't we do this more?
3. How would it benefit our group to compliment each other more?

Variation
In small groups, each person may create a trophy for every group member. Or you can divide the big group into two groups and each group can work together to create a trophy for each person on the other team.

Choices

Objective
For group members to talk about their perceptions of the group and about themselves.

Group Size
2 or more

Materials
➲ None

Description
Give group members a choice between two different things and ask them to select the thing that they feel best represents the group (or themselves). For example, say "When this group is making a decision, is it like (A) a river or (B) a lake?" Designate a place to stand on one side of the room for people who select A and on the other side of the room for people who select B. Once people make their choice, ask some members of the group to explain why they chose what they did. You may do several rounds of this with different choices to select from.

GROUP CHOICE IDEAS
When this group is making a decision is it like (A) a river or (B) a lake?
When this group must complete a task is it more like (A) a sloth or (B) a cheetah?
Would you describe your leadership skills as (A) a hammer (B) a nail?
Would you describe your following skills as (A) thunder (B) rain?
Would you say this group is (A) balanced (B) off balance?

Create more choices to fit your group's needs, issues, and experiences. Using a metaphor is a good way to get people talking about group dynamics in an indirect and non-threatening manner.

Group Labels

Objective
To talk about how we treat one another in the group.

Group Size
6 or more

Materials
- ➲ Sticky back labels
- ➲ Black marking pens

Description
To prepare for this activity, fill out sticky-back labels with titles (see list of suggestions below). Choose a game from the team-building chapter (Swamp Crossing, Water Transfer, Sneak-a-Peek, or Make a Meal work well), or you may choose any other game, such as volley-ball, basketball or even a board game. Before playing, put a label on each person's forehead or back. They must wear the label throughout the game, and people must treat them as they would treat someone with that label in real life. Don't let the players know what label they are wearing and others should not tell them what it is. After the game, give each person a chance to guess what label they were wearing and have them tell how it felt to be treated the way they were.

Different groups need to deal with different types of labels; you should fill out your labels based on your group's needs.

Corporate groups may have: boss, secretary, receptionist, client, complaining customer, etc.

Teenage groups may deal with cliques: jock, nerd, popular, druggie, cowboy, brain, etc.

This also works for different culture groups or society stigmas: Latino, Asian, African American, Caucasian, Jew, Christian, Muslim, woman, man, famous person, homeless person, person with AIDS, etc.

Discussion Prompts

1. How do you feel after this activity?
2. What surprised you the most?
3. Do you think that in our culture people treat others who are different from them differently? Why or why not?
4. How do these differences affect our group?

To You but from Who?

Objective
For group members to affirm one another in an indirect, fun manner.

Group Size
4 to 15 participants is ideal

Materials
- 1 envelope per person
- Paper
- Pens or pencils

Description
Give each person an envelope, pen or pencil, and several small slips of paper. Ask everyone to put their name on an envelope and then pass their envelope to the person sitting next to them.

Once you receive your neighbor's envelope, you write down an attribute that you admire about that person on a slip of paper. Add your name and then place the paper in the envelope. Continue passing the envelopes around until everyone has written down a comment for everyone else in the group.

Once all of the envelopes are full, they should be passed to the leader. The leader then selects one of the envelopes and selects a comment to read out loud to that person, without reading the name of the person who wrote it. The person whom the comment was written about will then try to guess who wrote the comment, and if they guess correctly, they receive a point. The object is to be the one with the most points in the end.

Go around the circle reading one comment from each envelope before starting over with the first person. Continue in this manner until all the comments are read from each person's envelope. After the game is finished, each person may collect their own envelope and keep it as a reminder of all their good qualities.

Discussion Prompts

1. How do you feel after hearing all those positive things about yourself?
2. Do you often hear positive things from others? How does this affect you? How does it affect the group?
3. Will you keep this envelope? Why or why not?
4. Why is it important for group members to affirm one another?

Variation

After everyone has written attributes down and filled the envelopes, redistribute the envelopes among the group members, so that each person takes turns reading a comment from the envelope that they have. This is simply a way to get everyone more involved in the process.

Question Cookies

Objective
To help the group open up in a fun and productive way.

Group Size
4 or more

Materials
- Fortune cookies (homemade or store bought)
- Tweezers
- Small slips of paper
- Pen or pencil

Description

Use fortune cookies as a way of asking group members different questions or as a way of getting them to share more openly. Do this by replacing the existing fortunes with your own questions or directions. To take an existing fortune out of a cookie, pull it out with tweezers very carefully. Write down a question, phrase or direction on a small slip of paper and slip it into the cookie. Or, you may leave the fortune in and simply add your own slip of paper with it. If you are feeling really ambitious you may make your own cookies!

Once you have all of your "question cookies" done, have the group sit in a circle and give each person a cookie. Go around the circle and allow group members to take turns opening their cookie and then following the directions or answering the question inside.

IDEAS FOR YOUR COOKIES

State three strengths of the group.

Give each of the five people to your right a compliment.

What is your best quality when you are working in a group?

Pick four people in the group to give you a compliment.

What is the best thing that happened to you when you were with this group?

Who is the first person you remember meeting in this group and why?

What thing about this group makes you laugh?

Name someone in the group who has good leadership skills and state why.

Name someone in the group who is the "glue" and state why.

Give the four people in the group who have a birthday closest to yours a compliment.

(You may create your own slips for your cookies or use more than one of each of these ideas for larger groups.)

Variation

Use this activity as a mixer with get to know you type questions inside.

Glory Story

Objective
For people to compliment each other and to share what they see as the positive traits of the group.

Group Size
2 or more

Materials
➲ Paper
➲ Pens or pencils

Description
Divide the group into small groups of one to six participants each. Separate the groups so that they cannot hear each other. Supply each group with a couple sheets of paper and a pen or pencil. Assign each group to one of the other groups and ask them to write down all of the names of the people from that other group on their paper.

Ask each group to write a story that includes all of the members of the other group as the characters, with each character in the story using his/her positive traits, strong points, and assets as a part of the story line. Once all of the stories are written, ask each group to read their story to the entire group.

Discussion Prompts
1. Were you surprised by any of the attributes that the other group gave to your character?
2. Can you think of any more positive traits that you would add to your character or to anyone else's character in the group?
3. How can you use your strong points to improve the group or to improve yourself?

Variation

Have each person write a story about themselves and add other members of their family, friends, or group members as the other characters.

Our House

Objective
For group members to share how they see others in the group and what role they think each person has on the team.

Group Size
6 to 20 is ideal

Materials
- Stack of 3x5 index cards
- Tape
- Scissors
- Pens or pencils
- Optional: Colored markers, glue

Description
This can be done individually or in small groups.

Give each group a stack of 3x5 index cards, tape, scissors and a pen or pencil. Each group must create a house out of the cards by taping, folding, cutting, or anything else they can think of to do to the cards in order to form a small model of a house.

Each person in the large group should somehow be represented in the construction of the house by having his/her name written on a part of the house that reflects his/her role in the group. Someone who is a good leader may be the foundation of the house. Someone who welcomes newcomers may be the door to the house. Besides just parts of the house, people may be items in the house, such as a comfortable chair, lamp, phone, etc.

Encourage groups or individuals to be creative and allow time for sharing once everyone has completed building their house.

Variation

Instead of building the houses, draw them on paper, and ask group members to write in different people in the places that represents them the best.

Be a Light

Objective
To talk about the group in a fun, descriptive, yet non-threatening manner.

Group Size
2 or more

Materials
◔ None

Description
Gather the group together and ask people to take turns answering the question: "If the light in our office (schoolroom, family room, therapy room, gym, etc.) could talk, what would it say about our group?" Do several rounds of this and replace the word "light" with different objects that the group comes in contact with frequently.

Discussion Prompts
Allow group members to ask questions about the answers given and hold a group discussion about any unusual or interesting answers.

Alphabetical List of Games

More Team-Building Activities
for Every Group

Alanna's newest book titled **More Team-Building Activities for Every Group** contains 107 more games and activities that promote team-building in an interactive and fun way. The games are new, different, experiential, exciting, easy to lead and require minimal resources.

Whatever group you work with will find **More Team-Building Activities for Every Group** to be a valuable resource that will help turn any group into a team!

Find sample games from both books on our web site
www.gamesforgroups.com

(Order form found on last page of this book.)

Two other great books
- By Alanna Jones

104 Activities That Build: Self-esteem, Teamwork, Communication, Anger Management, Self-discovery, and Coping skills

and

The wRECking Yard of games and activities

If you found *Team-Building Activities for Every Group* useful, helpful and informative, you'll love Alanna's other two books – *The wRECking Yard of games and activities,* and *104 Activities That Build:!*

Each book contains 104 more games and activities that are unique, fun and therapeutic. Both books cover the topics of teamwork, self-esteem, self-discovery, coping skills, communication, and anger management.

Each game is easy to use or adapt, teaches a lesson, and requires minimum resources. Teachers, counselors, therapists,   and youth workers across the country have found these books to be valuable resources that are growing quickly in popularity!

Find sample games from both books on our web site
www.gamesforgroups.com

(Order form found on last page of this book.)

Team Up

The team-building game you play with a group!

If your group liked the games in this team-building book, they will love the board game Team Up.

Team Up combines the fun of group initiative, problem solving and team-work activities with the simplicity of a creative new board game.

Team Up can be played in small teams of three or with a big group and teams as large as ten people each. Your team must work together each time it is your turn in order to win!

Team Up comes with a fold out game board, dice, playing pieces, thera-peutic discussion sheets, and 200 different activities that challenge any group — physically, mentally, and individually — to work for the good of the team.

This is a fun game for camp groups, therapy groups, corporate groups, and scouts, and it is great for use in any classroom. Any group that wants to grow closer together and learn by taking risks and being challenged, while at the same time laughing a lot and having fun, will enjoy the game Team Up!

Team Up comes in a easy to use 3 ring binder with everything you need included.

YOU CAN ORDER IT NOW FOR ONLY $29!

Ages 8 to adult
8 to 60 people (you may play with as few as 6)

(Order form found on last page of this book.)

Book and Game Order Form

TITLE	PRICE	QUANTITY	TOTAL
Team -Building Activities for	$16	_____	_____
More Team-Building Activities	$16	_____	_____
104 Activities That Build:	$24	_____	_____
The wRECking Yard	$24	_____	_____
Team Up (board game)	$29	_____	_____

Washington State residents add 8% sales tax _____

Shipping: $4 (no matter how many items you order!) _____

TOTAL [_____]

Name _____

Address _____

City _____ State _____ Zip_____

Telephone (_____)_____

Payment Type: Visa _____ Master Card_____Check _____ PO_____
Card number

_____

Expiration Date _____/_____ Name on card_____

Order by Fax, Phone or Mail to:
Rec Room Publishing
PO Box 404
Richland, WA 99352
PHONE (509) 946-7315   FAX (509)943-7629

e-mail: RecRoom@att.net
Web Page: www.gamesforgroups.com